LOVE ME SLENDER

LOVE ME SLENDER

by Vanessa Brooks

WARNER/CHAPPELL PLAYS

LONDON

A Warner Music Group Company

ACKNOWLEDGEMENT

Thanks to Connal Orton for the title.

DEDICATION

For my sister Fiona.

LOVE ME SLENDER was first presented on 24th September, 1996 at the Stephen Joseph Theatre, Scarborough, with the following cast:

SIOBHAN	Jenny Funnell
KELLY	Constance Barrie
CLAUDETTE	Sue Cleaver
ROSIE	Miriam Leake
LUCINDA	Emma Gregory
CELIA	Irene Sutcliffe
JEAN	Jill Brassington

Directed by Auriol Smith
Designed by Juliet Nichols
Lighting by Kath Geraghty

CHARACTERS

SIOBHAN
: 30s/40s. Group leader.
Target weight: Maintained it for two years
thank you and so will you.

CLAUDETTE
: 40s. Hotel bar manager. Mancunian.
Target weight: A turquoise mini skirt and
for my daughter not to be ashamed of me.

LUCINDA
: 30s. Marketing manager.
Target weight: 40K a year and an executive
chair.

ROSIE
: 30s. Church worker. Living with an ailing
mother.
Target weight: A slim third finger and that
one small word.

CELIA
: 60s. Retired housewife.
Target weight: Room in the waistband for
an extra post-bridge scone and room in my
husband's life for me.

JEAN
: 40s/50s. Part-time wife, mother and
chronic overworker.
Target weight: The confidence to make an
independent decision. I think.

KELLY
: 20s. Unemployed.
Target weight: Transparency.

Five scenes over a sixth month period at the St Jude's
Tunbridge Wells branch of the Slim for Life dieting club.

The action takes place in the changing room next to the
church hall.

ACT ONE

Scene One

Harvest festival.

*The ladies' cloakroom at St Jude's church hall, Tunbridge
Wells. A long low bench in the centre of the room. Benches at
the sides with pegs attached. A mirror. Discarded bags,
shoes, etc. A pile of hymn books. A row of small lockers. A
heater. A tatty rug.*

*Three exits. One leading into the church hall, one to the
kitchen, the other to the lavatories. The sound of bells
peeling and 'We Plough the Fields and Scatter' being played
on the organ in the adjacent church.*

KELLY *stands close to the pile of hymn books, pulling on two
bulky jumpers furtively.*

SIOBHAN	(*off*) Kelly — Kelly poppet, are you here? Kelly — I need you sweetheart . . . I NEED YOU — Kelly . . .
	(SIOBHAN *enters with coat, bag and umbrella. Damp but devastatingly attractive.*)
SIOBHAN	KELL — ah.
KELLY	What?
SIOBHAN	What are you doing?
KELLY	Nothing . . .
SIOBHAN	Good.
KELLY	I wasn't doing . . .
SIOBHAN	Set out the chairs for me, there's a poppet . . .
	(SIOBHAN *throws off her coat and sets down her bag.*)

KELLY   I was . . .

SIOBHAN   Running late . . .

KELLY   I was just . . .

SIOBHAN   Need to ask twice, do I?

KELLY   No.

             (KELLY *exits towards the hall*.)

SIOBHAN   (*shouting after* KELLY) And lay out a few
             intro-sheets on the trestle table — there's a
             batch of new girls in today.

             (SIOBHAN *finds a key in her handbag and opens
             a locker. She takes out a register and a cash
             box, unlocks it and deposits money from her
             purse and coat pocket. The church bell peels
             noon.*)

SIOBHAN   Hell's bells.

             (SIOBHAN *looks at her watch.*)

SIOBHAN   (*shouting towards the hall*) KELLY POPPET.
             HERE. NOW. KELLY. KELLY . . .

             (SIOBHAN *tots up the money in the box.* KELLY
             enters.)

KELLY   Yes?

SIOBHAN   The urn.

KELLY   Urn.

SIOBHAN   Urn. Yes. Go and stick the urn on, sweetheart.

KELLY   Urn. Right. Yes.

             (KELLY *exits towards the kitchen.* SIOBHAN
             rifles through money in the cash box.)

SIOBHAN   Oh no. Come on . . .

(SIOBHAN *tips her bag upside down on the bench and searches for loose coins.* KELLY *enters and heads towards the hall.*)

KELLY   Done it.

SIOBHAN   Uh-uh-uh-uh-uh.

KELLY   What?

SIOBHAN   S'il vous plait.

(SIOBHAN *doesn't look up but lifts a packet of toilet rolls out of her bag and hands them to* KELLY.)

SIOBHAN   Merci beaucoup.

(KELLY *takes the toilet rolls and exits towards the lavatories.* SIOBHAN *closes the lid on the cash box.*)

SIOBHAN   Damn it.

(KELLY *enters.* SIOBHAN *clutches the cash box to herself.*)

KELLY   Can I . . .

SIOBHAN   Sweetheart?

KELLY   Can I finish the chairs now?

SIOBHAN   Do anything for me, wouldn't you poppet?

KELLY   'Course.

(SIOBHAN *looks at herself in the mirror.*)

SIOBHAN   I don't suppose you could . . .

(SIOBHAN *turns to look at* KELLY.)

SIOBHAN   No. 'Course you couldn't.

KELLY   What? I can . . .

SIOBHAN   You can finish the chairs you can open the
               windows and you can give my desk a good
               dust down that's what you can do, OK?

KELLY   OK.

               (KELLY *exits towards the hall*.)

SIOBHAN   (*shouting after* KELLY) Polish in the drawer . . .
               there's a good girl . . .

               (SIOBHAN *stares at her reflection in the mirror,
               stands tall. Grins and stretches out a hand to
               herself*.)

SIOBHAN   There's a good girl.

               (SIOBHAN *breathes deeply*. CLAUDETTE *enters
               from the hall exit, dishevelled, lumpy and
               sodden in a heavy coat. She coughs and
               knocks on a bench*. SIOBHAN, *startled, notices
               her reflection*.)

SIOBHAN   Oh my . . .

CLAUDETTE   Sorry . . .

SIOBHAN   Pity's sake . . .

CLAUDETTE   Sorry . . .

SIOBHAN   What a fright . . .

CLAUDETTE   Sorry. Didn't mean to . . . I wonder if you can
               help me?

               (SIOBHAN *turns to face* CLAUDETTE.)

SIOBHAN   I'm sure I can.

CLAUDETTE   I am in the right place?

SIOBHAN   Yes. Yes you are.

CLAUDETTE   I'm looking . . . looking. Looking for . . .

SIOBHAN   I know what you're looking for.

CLAUDETTE   A meeting. I asked the girl out there but she just pointed, so I . . .

SIOBHAN   Our Kelly isn't a great conversationalist. A thinker. Not a talker.

CLAUDETTE   Oh. See . . .

SIOBHAN   Adorable.

CLAUDETTE   See I spoke . . .

SIOBHAN   Yes. Yes you did, didn't you sweetheart?

CLAUDETTE   Oh. Oh it's . . . it's you. You.

SIOBHAN   The one and only. Welcome. Welcome to the start of a whole new life.

             (SIOBHAN *pulls off her jumper to reveal a perfect figure.*)

SIOBHAN   What do you say to that then?

CLAUDETTE   Ta very much. Thought for a moment I might be barging into Bible reading . . .

             (SIOBHAN *searches in her bag.*)

SIOBHAN   As if.

CLAUDETTE   Yes. Or a confirmation class.

SIOBHAN   God forbid.

CLAUDETTE   Yes.

             (SIOBHAN *finds her sash and turns to face* CLAUDETTE.)

SIOBHAN   Get your coat off then.

CLAUDETTE   I beg your . . .

SIOBHAN	Sopping wet. Pop it off. Make yourself at home.

(SIOBHAN *scrutinises* CLAUDETTE *as she takes off her coat self-consciously.*)

SIOBHAN	Take a pew why don't you?

(CLAUDETTE *sits.* SIOBHAN *inspects herself in the mirror as she puts on her 'Achiever of the Year '94' sash.*)

CLAUDETTE	So. So you're the lady. You're the lady who . . .

(SIOBHAN *turns to face* CLAUDETTE.)

SIOBHAN	I am the lady who did. The lady who does. And the lady who will make sure you do likewise . . .
CLAUDETTE	Great.
SIOBHAN	Even if it kills me — OK?
CLAUDETTE	Wouldn't want that.
SIOBHAN	Glad to hear it. I'm Siobhan remember? Siobhan.

(SIOBHAN *attacks her hair with spray and a brush.*)

CLAUDETTE	Siobhan. Yes. 'Course I remember. 'Course. Oh my name's . . .
SIOBHAN	I know who you are.
CLAUDETTE	You do?
SIOBHAN	Knew the moment you walked in.

(CLAUDETTE *looks at herself in the mirror.*)

CLAUDETTE	Oh. My problem.
SIOBHAN	Your accent.

CLAUDETTE	Oh. Oh. Oh.
SIOBHAN	Yes.
CLAUDETTE	Sore thumb me.
SIOBHAN	Painful.
CLAUDETTE	I mean down here you can't help making an impact.
SIOBHAN	Certainly made an impact on me, poppet. The other night.
CLAUDETTE	Sorry. Was feeling a bit low.
SIOBHAN	Most people are when they call me.
CLAUDETTE	And once I'm set off I can't stop.
SIOBHAN	Frightening.
CLAUDETTE	Like a soda syphon with a jammed handle.
SIOBHAN	My line is awash with tears sweetheart. Lucky I keep a sponge on the telephone table. Girl like me could drown.
	(*A silence.*)
CLAUDETTE	I'm sorry.
SIOBHAN	Yes, alright.
	(SIOBHAN *applies make-up.*)
CLAUDETTE	Least you listened, I . . .
SIOBHAN	All part of the service.
CLAUDETTE	Sorry.
SIOBHAN	Apologise a lot, don't we Claudette?
CLAUDETTE	Do we? I . . .

SIOBHAN   Have to work on that.

CLAUDETTE   Will we?

SIOBHAN   Yes. Yes we will. I stopped saying sorry two
               years ago. Look good on it, don't I?

CLAUDETTE   Yes. You look. You look terrific.

SIOBHAN   You put your faith in me sweetheart. And
               tomorrow — you'll look terrific too — OK?

               (SIOBHAN *grasps* CLAUDETTE *by the shoulders.*)

CLAUDETTE   OK.

               (ROSIE *enters carrying two boxes of harvest
               festival produce and a notebook.* ROSIE'S *hair
               is very similar to* SIOBHAN'S.)

ROSIE   Siobhan. Siobhan would you . . .

SIOBHAN   Rosie. Rosie poppet.

               (SIOBHAN *kisses* ROSIE *on the cheek.* ROSIE
               juggles the boxes.)

SIOBHAN   Kissy-kissy. Missed you.

ROSIE   You too — kissy . . . would you mind if . . .

SIOBHAN   Rosie's my special girl, Claudette. She's here
               every week. On the dot. No worries with
               Rosie. Not supposed to have favourites but . . .
               well . . . I do enjoy our chats. Really.

ROSIE   Oh, me too.

SIOBHAN   Talk a lot between times, don't we?

ROSIE   You're always there for me, yes.

SIOBHAN   Become the best of friends, haven't we
               sweetheart?

ROSIE   } Yes. Yes of course.
SIOBHAN   (*to* CLAUDETTE) It's very friendly here. Say
               hello to Claudette.

ROSIE	Hello Claudette.
CLAUDETTE } ROSIE	Hello. Could I just bring a . . .
SIOBHAN	I love the hair. Love the hair. Love it.
ROSIE	Oh. Oh, do you?
SIOBHAN	Don't you love the hair, Claudette?
CLAUDETTE	Yes.
ROSIE	(*to* SIOBHAN) Do you really?
CLAUDETTE	Love it.
ROSIE	Really?
SIOBHAN	You went to Toppers? Like I said?
ROSIE	Yes Siobhan.
SIOBHAN	Good girl.
ROSIE	You're not just saying . . .
SIOBHAN	Very good girl.
ROSIE	I do look alright?
SIOBHAN	Good enough to eat. (*To* CLAUDETTE.) Yes?
CLAUDETTE } ROSIE	Yes. Only Laurence isn't very fond. In fact Laurence said it makes me look like . . .
SIOBHAN	What's all this then?
ROSIE	Just a couple? Couple of boxes? In here? Please? Pretty please?
SIOBHAN	(*looking at her watch*) It's nearly . . .
ROSIE	Please? All is safely gathered in but Laurence doesn't know quite where to put it.

(ROSIE *puts boxes on the centre bench.* SIOBHAN *gathers her belongings together.*)

SIOBHAN   Tell the Archbishop he's got you for ten minutes tops.

ROSIE   Wish you wouldn't call him that. Laurence is a Youth Worker, that's all. A vocation — taking orders — is something else ent . . .

SIOBHAN   Save it for the Sunday school, Rosie.

ROSIE   Just look at all of this.

CLAUDETTE   Lovely.

ROSIE   Laurence said everyone had been terribly generous this year.

SIOBHAN   This is Tunbridge Wells. It's not generosity. It's status.

ROSIE   Red letter day for my OAPs — tins of exotic fruit.

SIOBHAN   Yes. Can't afford the heating bill but never mind, there's mangoes in the larder.

ROSIE   It's . . . it's symbolic . . . Laurence says.

SIOBHAN   Laurence Laurence Laurence. He's a man Rosie. Not a god.

ROSIE   I know that, I . . .

SIOBHAN   Far from it, truth be told . . .

ROSIE   What do you . . .

SIOBHAN   Led you astray this week, has he?

ROSIE   NO. Well. Treats. The odd treat, he . . .

SIOBHAN   Oh, quelle surprise.

ROSIE	There was nothing I could . . .
SIOBHAN	Later. Want to stay here Claudette? I'll process new members after the regulars.

CLAUDETTE	What's going to happen? What do I . . .
ROSIE	Siobhan I . . .

SIOBHAN   (*to* CLAUDETTE) All in good time.

ROSIE   There've been some calls.

SIOBHAN   Calls. Right. Fine.

(SIOBHAN *exits towards the hall with cash box and register.*)

ROSIE   (*shouting towards hall*) Yes. Little pile of messages. On your desk, I . . . Dear. Dear, oh dear.

(ROSIE *finds a crate under a side bench, moves it to the centre bench and sorts through the box of goods making notes in a pad. A silence.*)

ROSIE   Sweet shop window?

CLAUDETTE   Sorry?

ROSIE   You look like a sweet shop window.

CLAUDETTE   Do I?

ROSIE   Either that or a soggy piece of paper stuffed under the windscreen wiper.

CLAUDETTE   I don't quite . . . Oh. Advert. I'm an advert. In the local paper.

ROSIE   Siobhan is splashing out. Still. Speculate to accumulate.

CLAUDETTE   I . . . I wondered what she'd look like. Siobhan. Gorgeous, isn't she?

ROSIE   Yes.

CLAUDETTE	Stunning.
ROSIE	Absolutely. Hard to believe she was once sixteen stone.
CLAUDETTE	Very.
ROSIE	She's a true inspiration. She can . . . I mean she can be a bit tough but it's all a front. And it's all for your own good, but I . . . I've seen the other side. She's . . . she's a Meltis Fruit.
CLAUDETTE	A what?
ROSIE	Soft centre. Brittle on the outside but syrupy in the middle.
CLAUDETTE	Life's one big boiled sweet to you, isn't it?
ROSIE	Yes. Unfortunately. Why do you think I'm here?
CLAUDETTE	How did she . . .
ROSIE	Oh no. My lips are zipped. Mustn't spoil it.
CLAUDETTE	Spoil what?
ROSIE	You'll get the full story. How she pulled herself up from the depths of despair. Triumphed over adversity. And married the man of her dreams. I'm following in her footsteps.
CLAUDETTE	Congratulations. When's the big day?
ROSIE	Don't know.
CLAUDETTE	Not decided?
ROSIE	No. Well. Laurence hasn't actually asked me yet.
CLAUDETTE	Ah.

ROSIE   But he will. Once I've hit target. Once I'm . . .
         do you mind?

         (ROSIE *passes boxes and packets to* CLAUDETTE
         to put into the crate.)

CLAUDETTE   What? Oh, oh no. Not at . . .

ROSIE   We're terrific friends. Laurence and I. We
         really are terrific friends. He gets on with
         Mummy too. And Mummy isn't easy. She's
         deaf. And rude. Well — to me. When she talks
         to me at . . . anyway. She's a bit wavy
         upstairs. But he charms her. I help him. With
         his work. Drive the minibus. Fold leaflets. I
         say to him, I say, you spread the word Laurence,
         I'll lick the stamps. They also serve who stand
         and salivate. I worship him. And he values my
         contribution. He said that once. But — well —
         I think he looks at me as — well — sort of . . .

CLAUDETTE   Free labour?

ROSIE   As a friend. Just a friend. Which is lovely but
         I keep — silly — but I keep wanting to — just
         — oh dear — have I gone pink?

CLAUDETTE   Why don't you tell him?

ROSIE   Couldn't. Couldn't possibly. I'm not right yet.
         Two stone to go.

CLAUDETTE   I'm sure it wouldn't matter to him if you were . . .

ROSIE   Oh but it does. It really does matter. I just
         don't measure up. I know I don't. Awhile ago.
         A while ago, well he touched me. Here. Just
         here. (*Touching cheek.*) He'd bought me an ice
         cream and there was raspberry sauce on my
         cheek. Went like that. (*Touching cheek.*) And
         he called me his little angel. His little angel
         with a dirty face. I said not so little. Not so
         little at all. And he said yes. Yes, he said.
         Shame about that.

CLAUDETTE	Should stop buying you cornets then, shouldn't he?
ROSIE	That's what Siobhan said. She doesn't like him very much.
CLAUDETTE	I don't think I'll be joining the fan club.
ROSIE	All I know is that I'm dizzy when he's close. That I can't breathe and that I keep going blinking pink. AARGH. Quite sick with it all. Have you ever felt like that?
CLAUDETTE	Feel like that right now.
	(CLAUDETTE *stands and looks out towards the hall.*)
CLAUDETTE	Can't believe I'm here. I spent half an hour dithering about at the end of the drive like an idiot. Nearly didn't come.
ROSIE	I was nervous too, the first time.
CLAUDETTE	I just hope there's someone here who's fatter than I am.
ROSIE	No, no, no. Ssh. Ssh.
CLAUDETTE	What?
ROSIE	(*whispering*) Taboo word. No one here is fat.
CLAUDETTE	(*whispering*) Oh. Sorry.
ROSIE	Everyone here is improving themselves. Siobhan says fat is a negative. Fat is admitting defeat. Siobhan says fat is reaching for another pork pie because it just doesn't matter any more.
CLAUDETTE	Siobhan's got all the answers, hasn't she?
ROSIE	No. But she does ask the right questions. Yummy. Mallow biscuits. Give me strength.

(LUCINDA *enters in mac, with umbrella.*)

LUCINDA   Hi — The lady said to come through. This is
            St Jude's? Someone's painted Michael Jackson
            over the board outside.

ROSIE   Slim for Life?

LUCINDA   Not yet. But I live in hope.

            (SIOBHAN *enters clutching a piece of paper.*
            LUCINDA *takes off her coat and hangs it up.*)

SIOBHAN   Did you take all these messages Rosie?

ROSIE   What?

SIOBHAN   Why aren't they coming? Why? Why?

ROSIE   Well. I . . .

SIOBHAN   This is most of the group.

ROSIE   I know. I know. I . . .

SIOBHAN   Did you talk to them? Did you talk to Sandra
            and Mary and . . .

ROSIE   No. Laurence did.

SIOBHAN   What? Laurence did what?

ROSIE   They called the vicarage to find out the new
            time and . . . Laurence just happened to be
            there and he . . .

SIOBHAN   Well what on earth did he say to them Rosie?

ROSIE   I . . .

SIOBHAN   Yes?

ROSIE   Laurence does feel. Well . . .

SIOBHAN   Yes? Yes?

ROSIE   Well. Well. Well he feels that Sunday pursuits
                     aren't convenient for a lot of . . .

SIOBHAN   I know exactly how Laurence feels about
                     Sunday 'pursuits'. That's what bothers me.

ROSIE   Oh but I'm sure really sure that he wouldn't
                     say anything . . .

SIOBHAN   And why is he putting boxes on my trestle?

ROSIE   Oh he isn't — he hasn't — I'll sort it out —
                     silly silly . . .

                     (ROSIE *exits*.)

SIOBHAN   (*shouting after* ROSIE) I'm all for God and that
                     sweetheart, but he does get in the way of my
                     meetings. You must be Lucinda — yes?

LUCINDA   That's right. I called the day before . . .

SIOBHAN   Welcome poppet. Just sit tight. Won't be long.
                     OK?

                     (SIOBHAN *exits towards the hall*.)

CLAUDETTE   Hello. Claudette.

LUCINDA   Hi. So. What's the form?

CLAUDETTE   Search me. I'm new too. Just have to wait.

                     (LUCINDA *looks in the mirror as she takes off
                     her coat*.)

LUCINDA   I hope it's not ritual humiliation. I'm not very
                     good at these group things. I once joined a
                     map reading class and had to leave because
                     the tutor kept waving my D-minuses in the air
                     and calling me Mark Thatcher.

CLAUDETTE   Siobhan seems alright.

LUCINDA   Well she looks thin. That's good enough for
                     me.

(LUCINDA *looks at her side view in the mirror.*)

LUCINDA   Mirror mirror on the wall, who's the fattest cow of all?

CLAUDETTE   Me. Hands down. And you're not allowed to say fat apparently. Rule number one.

(CELIA *enters covered from head to foot in waterproof clothing and wearing a hat and Wellington boots.*)

CELIA   Hello. I was told to come and join my fellow new girls. I'm Celia. Sixty four and a half. Addicted to fruit scones. And totally bonkers.

LUCINDA } Oh.
CLAUDETTE } What?

CELIA   To be here I mean. Must say I feel distinctly odd. I've never done anything like this before.

CLAUDETTE } Neither have I.
LUCINDA } Me neither.

CELIA   Little nervous, truth be told.

CLAUDETTE } Likewise.
LUCINDA } Me too.

CELIA   Still. They say confession is good for the soul. Let's hope it's good for the waistline, too.

(CELIA *peels off her layers.* LUCINDA *applies make-up, looking in the mirror.*)

LUCINDA   I just need to lose ten pounds by the New Year or I won't stand a cat in hell's chance of a promotion.

CELIA   Why? Are you a fashion model?

LUCINDA   I'm up for second to the chief executive. He sacked his last deputy because her collarbone

disappeared and she stopped looking like a
coat hanger.

CLAUDETTE   That's outrageous. Mr Universe, is he?

LUCINDA   Five foot two. Beer belly and a dome like a
                 gobstopper but he is the boss.

CELIA   I didn't think you could get away with that
                 sort of thing nowadays.

LUCINDA   He's clever. Finds excuses. But it's common
                 knowledge. He has this test. Any female up for
                 a job in his department has to walk between
                 the filing cabinet and his desk. He's measured
                 the gap. Perfect size ten hips. He spots an inch
                 of flesh bulging over his mahogany and that's
                 it. You're out.

CELIA   How awful. But at least someone is looking
                 over.

LUCINDA   What on earth do you mean?

CELIA   Well the last time I remember my husband
                 passing any comment on my appearance was
                 in . . . yes. Yes. Must have been back in
                 nineteen eighty nine.

                 (CELIA *struggles with her boots.*)

CLAUDETTE   Had you been on a diet?

CELIA   No. My hair had turned orange. A bad perm.
                 Plus Ted lives for his fry-ups. I die for them.
                 I'm married to a weight problem. I wonder if
                 you can liberate me?

CLAUDETTE }   Sorry?
LUCINDA   What? Oh . . .

                 (CELIA *holds out her Wellington-encased feet.*
                 CLAUDETTE *and* LUCINDA *help to pull the boots
                 off.*)

CELIA   Been rambling. New hobby. George is a fitness
               fanatic.

LUCINDA   I thought Ted was your . . .

CELIA   Oh George is a friend. We met him at the
               RAAFA Club. Marvellous chap. Sixty nine
               and fit as a fiddle. He runs three miles before
               breakfast and bungee jumps. Super-fit is
               George.

CLAUDETTE   Wish I was.

               (CLAUDETTE *and* LUCINDA *struggle with the
               boots.*)

CELIA   We're all planning an excursion to the
               Pyrenees. A walking holiday. I'm very excited.
               Always wanted to travel. So we're in training.
               Now Ted's fine — the wiry type — but I puff
               behind with the mint cake like the proverbial
               pack horse. This donkey needs to lighten her
               load.

               (CLAUDETTE *and* LUCINDA *remove the boots.*)

CLAUDETTE   And invest in some bigger boots.

               (CLAUDETTE *looks out towards the hall.* CELIA
               finds shoes in her bag and puts them on.)

CELIA   Had to leave them to it this morning. Can't
               keep up.

CLAUDETTE   Somebody tell me I'm hallucinating.

               (CELIA *and* LUCINDA *join* CLAUDETTE *looking
               out towards the hall.*)

CELIA   ⎫   Scales.
LUCINDA   ⎬   Scales.
CLAUDETTE ⎭   Scales . . . You don't think . . . I mean . . . it's
               not broadcast, is it? I don't think I could bear
               to hear a load of strangers gasping.

CELIA   Ten stone seven.

LUCINDA   Just over ten.

                 (*A silence.*)

CLAUDETTE   Just over ten . . . big boned. Prone to water
                 retention . . . Oh God knows — I'm frigging
                 terrified.

CELIA   I don't think we need be too fearful.

CLAUDETTE   Just don't fancy stepping on the scales in front
                 of a roomful of stick insects.

CELIA   There's only three of them here.

CLAUDETTE   None of them look that — well — you know.

LUCINDA   But that's a good sign.

CELIA   Yes. It must work.

ALL   Yes.

                 (*They move away from the exit.*)

CLAUDETTE   Better work. I . . . I've only got a couple of
                 months. I'm visiting my daughter. Katy. She's
                 at university. We don't talk as much as I'd
                 like and I . . . I just want . . . just have to
                 make a good impression for once.

CELIA   I'm sure you will.

CLAUDETTE   Plus my job isn't helping me. I manage the bar
                 up at the Queens Hotel. It's hard to turn down
                 five star meals when they're gratis.

CELIA   So how does it actually work? She was very
                 vague on the phone. What do we have to do?

CLAUDETTE   It's a mystery.

LUCINDA   I'll try anything. Pretty desperate, to be
                 honest.

CLAUDETTE   Snap.

CELIA   Well Siobhan looks pencil thin and pushy.
                 Just the type to keep one on the straight and
                 narrow.

                 (SIOBHAN *enters followed by* JEAN, *carrying
                 umbrella and shoulder bag.*)

SIOBHAN   Okey dokey ladies. I'd like you to meet Jean.
                 Jean is no stranger to success.

CLAUDETTE   ⎫   Hello.
CELIA   ⎪   Good morning.
LUCINDA   ⎬   Hi.
JEAN   ⎭   Hello. Nice to . . .

SIOBHAN   Give them a twirl sweetheart.

JEAN   Twirl.

SIOBHAN   Yes.

JEAN   Oh should I?

SIOBHAN   Yes.

JEAN   Shall I? Can I? Do I dare?

SIOBHAN   Twirl Jean, twirl.

JEAN   Oooh.

                 (JEAN *twirls.*)

SIOBHAN   Jean came to me looking like an earth mother.
                 Four stone down and she's in the market for
                 yogic flying, aren't you poppet?

CLAUDETTE   ⎫   Very good.
CELIA   ⎬   Four stone.
LUCINDA   ⎭   Not bad at all.

JEAN   Am I?

SIOBHAN   Yes. Yes you are.

JEAN   You've come to the right club. This lady is a
                miracle worker.

SIOBHAN   Good girl.

                (JEAN *rummages through her shoulder bag*.)

SIOBHAN   If you'd like to go through, Kelly will tick you
                off in the register. Sort out your subs.

LUCINDA   OK.
CELIA   Ah — yes.
CLAUDETTE   Oh. Just find my . . .

                (*All find their purses.*)

SIOBHAN   I'll be along in a mo to give you your
                dietpacks and to weigh you in. Off you pop . . .

CLAUDETTE   Yes.
LUCINDA   Right.
CELIA   Here goes.
SIOBHAN   Come on — be happy. New life around the
                corner. Greet it with a smile — yes?

                (CLAUDETTE, LUCINDA *and* CELIA *exit*.)

SIOBHAN   Jean. So embarrassed.

JEAN   Don't be.

SIOBHAN   Had it in an envelope on the kitchen table. I
                said Simes. I said first of the month. Don't let
                me forget the rent for the hall I said.

JEAN   He is a busy man, Siobhan.

SIOBHAN   Can say that again. Say to him sometimes say
                that restaurant sees more of you than I do.
                Still, can't complain. Business is booming.
                Booming.

JEAN   Fifty pounds do it?

SIOBHAN	Won't leave you short?
JEAN	Oh no. Lots of money today. Lots. Been paid for my cleaning. And the assistant teaching and the care work at the old people's home.
SIOBHAN	Be sweeping chimneys next won't you.
JEAN	But you said it was the right thing to do.
SIOBHAN	Yes. It is.
JEAN	I mean I have my own money now and I . . .
SIOBHAN	Absolutely. We don't want Gregory treating you like a doormat again do we?
JEAN	You are sure it's the right . . .
SIOBHAN	Fifty pounds you said.
JEAN	Fifty pounds. Yes. Of course.

(SIOBHAN *takes the money*.)

SIOBHAN	Something tells me you're going to hit target this morning, Jean. I'm thrilled for you. You're nearly there sweetheart. At the mountain top.
JEAN	It's the descent I'm worried about.
SIOBHAN	No descent this time. Flight. Flight. Believe me. And every time a member hits target my wings get a little extra lift.
JEAN	Let's hope I send you soaring into the cosmos then.
SIOBHAN	You'll be flying with me sweetheart. On the maintenance plan.

(SIOBHAN *heads towards the hall*.)

JEAN	Siobhan. I . . . I . . . I . . .

SIOBHAN	Jean?
JEAN	I can't, I . . . I can't just can't make up my mind.
SIOBHAN	You never can poppet. That's what I'm here for.
JEAN	You see I can't . . .
SIOBHAN	Make up your mind about what?
JEAN	I could — I mean I should . . .
SIOBHAN	Could what sweetheart?
JEAN	And one minute I think yes —
SIOBHAN	Jean.
JEAN	Then I think no and it gets terribly . . .
SIOBHAN	Meeting to get on with . . .
JEAN	I can't make up my mind. About Gregory. About whether to tell him or not. About my little . . .
SIOBHAN	Treat.
JEAN	Betrayal.
SIOBHAN	Experiment.
JEAN	Affair. Oh God what am I . . .
SIOBHAN	You were trying out your new body Jean. That's all. OK? It was scientific. Not emotional. I understand that. But husbands get all worked up about these things. You don't need it sweetheart. Not with your nerves. Do not tell Gregory. OK?
JEAN	Scientific. Not emotional.
SIOBHAN	Yes.

JEAN	Do not tell Gregory.

SIOBHAN No. Now come on. Time for the weigh-in.

JEAN Just a second. Every little counts. This cardigan weighs heavy.

(JEAN *peels off some clothes.*)

JEAN Not many in this week. The hall looks quite empty.

SIOBHAN But very welcoming. Now we're a Laurence-free zone.

JEAN Rosie seemed a little upset.

SIOBHAN All I did was send him packing. You'd think I'd burned him at the stake. He's no good for her.

JEAN For her weight, certainly.

SIOBHAN He's devious, Jean. Manipulative. I know his game.

JEAN And she is quite naive.

SIOBHAN Just the way he likes them I'm sure. I can see it happening and I just don't want — I'm very fond of her and I don't want her to make the same mistakes as . . .

JEAN Mistakes? You?

SIOBHAN What — Oh — I . . .

(KELLY *enters with register and subs box.*)

SIOBHAN Everything alright Kelly?

(KELLY *kneels at the bench and sorts through the money.*)

SIOBHAN 'Yes Siobhan.' 'I shall now count through the subs and make sure that all is in order.' If you

don't start asserting yourself poppet you'll
never get a job. When I have the time you and
I are going to sit down and . . .

(ROSIE *enters with another box of goods.*)

ROSIE   It's the last one.

(ROSIE *thumps the box onto the centre bench.*)

ROSIE   It has to be done Siobhan. Whether Laurence
               is here or not it has to be done.

SIOBHAN   (*to* JEAN) You go through poppet.

ROSIE   Food for the needy.

JEAN   Here goes.

ROSIE   The needy.

JEAN   Fingers crossed.

(JEAN *exits.*)

ROSIE   Sorry . . . I'm sorry, but some things are more
               important than Slim for Life.

(ROSIE *clutches a packet of biscuits.* SIOBHAN
approaches her.)

SIOBHAN   Only one thing is more important than Slim
               for Life, Rosie. You. And helping you to be
               happy. That's what I want sweetheart. Really.
               Can Laurence say the same?

(SIOBHAN *takes the biscuits from* ROSIE *and
puts them back in the box. She exits towards
the hall.* ROSIE *looks at* KELLY. KELLY *looks
down.*)

ROSIE   I'm not looking forward to the weigh-in. I
               think I may have put a couple on. Again.

(*The sound of clapping from the hall.* KELLY
and ROSIE *look in that direction.*)

ROSIE   Time for the welcome hugs. Probably an
                 American idea. Hug a lot Americans, don't
                 they? Mummy says it's because they wash
                 more often than we do. And use less public
                 transport . . . Kelly . . .

                 (ROSIE *moves closer to* KELLY.)

ROSIE   Siobhan'll be furious won't she . . .

                 (KELLY *picks up the register and subs box and
                 moves away from* ROSIE.)

ROSIE   I've had five double chocolate milkshakes this
                 week. Four fudge fingers and a family bag of
                 buttons.

                 (*The sound of a bell ringing in the hall and
                 applause.*)

ROSIE   Oh Jean's hit target. You can't be far off.
                 Follow the plan don't you. To the letter. Kelly,
                 can I talk to you — please . . .

                 (KELLY *moves farther away from* ROSIE *and
                 turns her back on her.*)

ROSIE   Laurence wants me to leave. He wants me to
                 leave the club. He doesn't like Siobhan. Says
                 she has a suspicious nature and that there's
                 nothing more destructive than a suspicious
                 nature. Says if I have any feeling for him I
                 have to leave. And she shouted at him just
                 now . . . What shall I do? What do you think
                 — should I go? Should I . . .

KELLY   LEAVE ME ALONE . . .

                 (JEAN *enters from the hall.*)

JEAN   You are looking at a target-hitting gold star
                 slimmer.

(CELIA, CLAUDETTE *and* LUCINDA *enter,
absorbed in their dietpacks.*)

JEAN   Kelly — Rosie — Siobhan wants you for
                your . . .

                (KELLY *exits rapidly into the hall.*)

ROSIE   No. Kelly — don't tell Siobhan, please don't . . .

JEAN   Weigh-in. Tea is in the kitchen, ladies.

CELIA   Lovely. Er — it's Rosie, isn't it?

LUCINDA   Great.

                (LUCINDA *exits into the kitchen.* CLAUDETTE
                slumps on a bench with her dietpack.)

ROSIE   What? Oh — yes. Celia? You used to come to
                church.

CELIA   Oh, still do dear. (*Indicates her heart.*) In
                here. Where it counts.

                (CELIA *exits into the kitchen.*)

JEAN   Rosie. Siobhan's expecting you. Time to put
                your week on the scales.

                (ROSIE *exits towards the hall.* JEAN *finds bottle
                of mineral water in her bag.*)

JEAN   Shell-shocked?

CLAUDETTE   I've been kidding myself. I can't believe I
                weigh so much. I'll never do it.

JEAN   Of course you will.

CLAUDETTE   I can't help it you know. Being f — whatever.
                It's my glands.

JEAN   No it isn't.

CLAUDETTE	It's genetic then. I'm from Manchester. I was born screaming for a bacon butty and I haven't stopped.
JEAN	Tut-tut. Excuses.
CLAUDETTE	It's just I've tried so many times before . . .

(CLAUDETTE *looks at herself in the mirror.*)

| CLAUDETTE | I've spent half my life starving and look at me. I'm still a tub of lard. |

(LUCINDA *enters from the kitchen with tea cup, clutching dietpack.*)

LUCINDA	There's a month's reading in here.
JEAN	Siobhan's talked me out of the fridge on many an occasion. She's changed my life. She's very . . . knowing. You just have to trust her.
LUCINDA	Are you on a percentage or something?
JEAN	I'm on faith. Just believe. It works.

(CELIA *enters from the kitchen with tea cup and dietpack.*)

CELIA	Jean. What are all these photocopied sheets at the back?
JEAN	That's Siobhan's lifeplan. An innovation of hers. Fascinating stuff. Wait and . . .

(SIOBHAN *enters with arm around* ROSIE.)

| SIOBHAN | Lovely. You've found the tea. Time to find me. Pop yourself down Rosie. And don't fret, OK? I've asked Kelly to set us up for sin-bags and dieting diaries . . . |

(ROSIE *sits.*)

LUCINDA	What?
CELIA	Sin-bags?
CLAUDETTE	What's that?

SIOBHAN   All will be revealed. But I thought we could kick off in here nice and informal while we finish up our drinks. OK, Rosie? OK?

(ROSIE *nods*.)

SIOBHAN   Now I know we're all feeling a little bit tense. A touch scared. Do you all feel a bit scared?

CELIA	Yes.
CLAUDETTE	Yes. I am.
LUCINDA	Wondering what it's all . . .

SIOBHAN   Well you can all relax and take your fingernails out of the side of the bench because there is absolutely nothing to be afraid of and that's a promise, OK?

CELIA	Yes.
LUCINDA	OK.
CLAUDETTE	Alright.
SIOBHAN	Certainly not from me. Jean can be a bit ratty when she's crossed . . .

| JEAN | Oh please. |
| SIOBHAN | But I am not a slave driver. OK? There is no whip in my handbag. |

JEAN   Not what I've heard.

SIOBHAN   Been talking to my Simes have you?

JEAN   Don't need to, I can tell.

SIOBHAN   Well don't go telling him. He'll get ideas, eh? Eh everybody? (*Winking at* JEAN.) Bless you, poppet.

(*All laugh nervously*. SIOBHAN *laughs too much*.)

SIOBHAN   Lovely. Good to have a laugh, isn't it? And we
                   do laugh here — often — isn't that right
                   girls?

JEAN   }   Oh yes.
ROSIE   Yes Siobhan.

SIOBHAN   But. And this is a big 'but'. One thing I will
                   not have is unproductive behaviour in my
                   group — OK? I want hard work and I want
                   results, yes? I am deadly serious on this one.
                   Anyone displaying the wrong attitude and —
                   Jean?

JEAN   Asked to leave . . .

SIOBHAN   Yeah.

JEAN   Told to go . . .

SIOBHAN   That's right . . .

JEAN   Shown the door.

SIOBHAN   Shown . . . The . . . Door. It's happened. And
                   it's not pleasant, is it?

JEAN   No. No it's not.

SIOBHAN   I say to them I say don't waste my time don't
                   waste your time but most importantly don't
                   waste the group's time, our precious time. I
                   want light entertainment I have the television
                   thank you, I want a natter I call my friends, I
                   want to take the mickey and snigger and
                   backstab I take it elsewhere — yeah? So.
                   Now's your chance. Anyone who feels they
                   might be incapable of lending support of
                   taking the aims and goals of this group
                   seriously of really really achieving something
                   here then pick up your things right now full
                   refund pick up your things this minute and go.
                   Just leave. There's the door. Because we don't
                   want you here.

(*A silence.*)

SIOBHAN   Good. Commitment, ladies. Commitment.
               Stage one in the lifeplan.

               (SIOBHAN *takes dietpack from* LUCINDA *and
               holds up a copy of her lifeplan.*)

               You have made a commitment to the group, a
               commitment to me and most importantly a
               commitment to yourselves — yes?

               (*A silence.*)

               I know your history. Inside out. OK? Up,
               down, swings, roundabouts, an endless zig zag
               of gain and loss. I know your history ladies
               because it's mine, too. But I broke free. It's
               time for you to break free too. How long do
               your diets last? Do they ever really start? I'll
               do it tomorrow you say and tomorrow becomes
               the next day and the next week and the next
               month and before you know it you've gained
               two stone and lost your self-esteem, yes?
               Ladies your diet starts now — this minute —
               and it never stops, because it's not just a diet
               it's a way of life, a lifeplan that lies in your
               hands, written from my heart, yes? So.
               Commitment. Stage one. Congratulations.
               Congratulations to you all.

               (*A silence.*)

               After commitment comes discipline.
               Discipline. Eyes fixed on your goal, the goal
               you've strived for for years, you'll struggle,
               you'll feel weak and you'll be tempted —
               tempted by others, tempted by yourself because
               of all these demons in pretty little wrappers . . .

               (SIOBHAN *picks up goods from* ROSIE'S *box.*)

               Because lying on the bed is more comfy than
               going for a job — oh yes — because there are

times when letting go is easier than holding
on — holding on to what you really want —
because of all this it will be hard, it will be
very hard, it will be hell, but this time — this
time I am here for you, OK? Me. I am going to
haunt you ladies, I will be at the end of your
phone, I will be at the bottom of your dinner
plate, I will be in your oven and in your
training shoes making sure that you have that
discipline, yes? Discipline. Stage two.

(*A silence.*)

So you've made a commitment, you have
acquired discipline, the next stage on your
journey is sacrifice. Hard cold sacrifice. But
sacrifices have to be made, hmm? (*To*
LUCINDA.) The drinks after work. (*To* JEAN.)
The high-calorie veggie snacks. (*To* CELIA.)
The afternoon teas. (*To* CLAUDETTE.) The mid-
morning buns. (*To* ROSIE.) The lover from
cocoa mass hell. Kiss them all goodbye.

(*A silence.*)

And then the day comes when you wake up to
a glorious realisation. Stage four. Realisation.
You reach target. You have the body you
deserve and feel the satisfaction of a battle
well won. But after that joy, that triumph,
realisation ladies. Yes, the cycle has been
broken; yes, bad habits have been thrown away
and food is no longer a master but a servant;
but there has to be the realisation. The
realisation of the fact that you can only live
happily, healthily and free if you continue to
follow the plan.

(*A silence.*)

And finally. Stage five. Salvation. Mine was a
lonely war. One I wouldn't wish on anybody.
There was no one there for me. I lost seven
stone. Seven stone. Think about that for a

moment. Imagine it. From this — to this.
(*Indicating size.*) I'd always had problems.
From the year dot. Problems made flesh. And I
hated them. I hated myself so I shed that
person. That person who I despised. That
reminder of the heartache and the tears and
underneath I found everything I dreamed of.
Yes. From the small things — a wardrobe full
of clothes that fit, a thrill every time I slip
into a swimsuit — to the big things. A
beautiful home. A job that fulfils me. And a
man who I love who can find no fault with me
. . . Salvation because I am the best I can be.
And I want that for you. Well it's here. It's
here for the taking, ladies.

(SIOBHAN *waves the lifeplan.*)

Commitment. Discipline. Sacrifice.
Realisation and salvation. Let's get to work.
It'll take time. Weeks. Maybe months, but it's
worth it. Believe me, it's worth it. Remember
— not slim for today, not slim for tomorrow,
but . . .

ALL	Slim for life.
SIOBHAN	Can't hear you. Not slim for tomorrow, but . . .

ALL	SLIM FOR LIFE.
SIOBHAN	GO. GO. GO. GO. GO. GO. MOVE. Take your tea through.

(CELIA, LUCINDA, KELLY *and* JEAN *exit into the hall.*)

SIOBHAN   And leave the hot seat at the front free for
Rosie. She's had a bad week. Needs a lot of
support. A lot of support sweetheart — OK?

CLAUDETTE Could I just get a cup of . . .

SIOBHAN   Quickly then. Work to be done. Run. Chop
chop chop.

CLAUDETTE   Yes. Won't be a . . . Chop chop.

                   (SIOBHAN *claps her hands behind* CLAUDETTE,
                   who runs into the kitchen.)

SIOBHAN   I don't care about Laurence, Rosie, Laurence
                   means nothing to me. He doesn't exist. I care
                   about you. Now. You're stuck on discipline.
                   It's time to move on to sacrifice. OK? Is that
                   OK?

ROSIE   Yes.

SIOBHAN   Good girl. Go.

ROSIE   ⎫   Yes. Yes.
SIOBHAN   ⎭   Go. Go.

                   (ROSIE *exits towards the hall, bumping into*
                   KELLY *who enters.*)

ROSIE   ⎫   Excuse me.
KELLY   ⎭   Sorry.

SIOBHAN   Kelly — where you off to? I want your diary
                   first. You lost three pounds this week. I want
                   the new girls to hear from a winner.

                   (KELLY *indicates towards the lavatories.*)

SIOBHAN   Hurry up then. Hurry up.

                   (SIOBHAN *exits towards the hall.* KELLY *makes*
                   towards the lavatories then stops, lifts up her
                   jumper and deposits several hymn books from
                   her waistband on to the pile. CLAUDETTE *enters*
                   from the kitchen with a tea cup.)

CLAUDETTE   ⎫   What are you . . .
KELLY   ⎭   Nothing. Nothing.

                   (KELLY *heads towards the hall exit. Blackout.*)

Scene Two

A wedding. One month later.

The same. The sound of bells peeling and 'Love Divine All Loves Excelling' being played on the organ in the adjacent church.

Claudette, half-dressed in workout clothes, stands on a side bench looking out. Kelly sits huddled in a heavy jumper. Lucinda and Jean change into workout clothes, watching Celia dressed in a tracksuit who groans as she demonstrates a stretching exercise.

Lucinda	Are you sure you should be doing that?
Jean	Yes. Yes, Celia. Do be careful.
Celia	Easy peasy, pudding and pie. George taught me. It's for suppleness, apparently.
Lucinda	George sounds exhausting.
Celia	He's a marvel. Fantastic company, too. He comes around every evening to supervise Ted and me jigging about on the uppy-downy machine.
Jean	The what?
Lucinda	Step machine.
Celia	It's working. With my weight loss and my fitness programme I'll definitely be able to keep up with the boys.
Claudette	I've heard of a shotgun wedding but the mechanism must have been jammed on this one.
Celia Lucinda Jean	} Honestly. Claudette. Really.

CLAUDETTE   Sorry. But she's ready to drop.

CELIA   Please. Let's not be vulgar.

CLAUDETTE   Not vulgar. Fact of life. I was up the duff with Katy the first time I was wed.

               (CLAUDETTE *steps off the bench and continues changing.*)

JEAN   'With child'. You mean you were 'with child'.

CLAUDETTE   'With child'. Make me sound like the Virgin Mary.

LUCINDA   That would be a miracle.

CELIA   Just how many times have you been married?

CLAUDETTE   Three. Thought the last one would be lucky. Pathological liar. Discovered he had half a dozen aliases and a couple of extra wives. He ran off with a chambermaid and most of my sanity. Never again.

CELIA   For all the pain you have your daughter. And that's a blessing.

CLAUDETTE   I wish she felt the same way about me.

JEAN   Gregory thought we should renew our vows. Last summer.

LUCINDA   } That's nice.
CLAUDETTE   } Ah.
CELIA   } Oh lovely.

JEAN   No. I put him off. Didn't feel right. Because I . . . maybe one day. I'd like that. I think. Perhaps.

CELIA   Ted and I were married here.

LUCINDA   } This church?
JEAN   } Really?

CELIA	Yes. Proper church wedding. Very proper church then. Back in the days when the ceremony meant more than videotape and the vows were more important than the cake.
LUCINDA	Well if I ever get married . . .
CLAUDETTE	Oh yes. Who is he?
LUCINDA	I haven't met him yet. But if I did. If I do — Registry office. No fuss. He'll say what he has to say, I'll say what I have to say . . . and then do my best to avoid the buffet table.
CLAUDETTE	You romantic you. Girls. What do you think? I wouldn't have dared a month ago.

(CLAUDETTE *admires herself in the mirror.*)

JEAN	You look great.
CELIA	Marvellous.
CLAUDETTE	Not quite the green goddess but I'm getting there. Siobhan's been wonderful. I had to call her three times this past week.
JEAN	You had a rough ride?
CLAUDETTE	Monday I was in serious danger of seduction by a plate of venison sausages.
LUCINDA	Lethal.
CELIA	Very fatty.
CLAUDETTE	On Wednesday I found my finger in a sherry trifle.
JEAN	Dangerous.
CLAUDETTE	And last night my willpower totally collapsed. I very nearly tucked in to the leftovers from a fourteen course banquet. After Eights and all. Bless her, Siobhan was so good. Reminded me of my trip. What I want to achieve. The voice of my conscience.

(LUCINDA *puts her clothes away in a locker.*)

LUCINDA   Yes. Very loud voice. Persistent, too.

(*All stare at* LUCINDA.)

LUCINDA   What? Look — you know I missed a meeting
               the other week. Couldn't help it. Have to show
               willing if I stand a chance for this job. Well. I
               got back home. Eleven at night and the phone
               rings and it was Siobhan. She asked me if I
               was thinking of having a drink. Just like that.
               Told me booze was my enemy. Not to do it. I
               know the odd G and T has been a problem but
               she made me feel like an alcoholic and I
               thought — I just thought it was a bit . . . Why
               are you all staring at me?

CELIA   You had no intention of having a drink?

LUCINDA   I had the bottle in my hand but that's not —

CELIA   It is your downfall food, dear.

CLAUDETTE   Wasted calories.

LUCINDA   Just annoyed me slightly because . . .

JEAN   She was right.

LUCINDA   Yes. OK.

JEAN   She always is. That's her gift. I think.

LUCINDA   And she did stop me. And I know I lack.

ALL   Discipline.

LUCINDA   Mea culpa.

(LUCINDA *steps on to the bench and looks out.*)

JEAN   Just wait 'til you get on to realisation.

CLAUDETTE   It's sacrifice that gives me chills.

LUCINDA   I think the horse and carriage was a mistake.
               The bride can't get in. The driver's giving her
               a leg up.

               (CLAUDETTE *crosses to* KELLY.)

CLAUDETTE   You not getting changed Kelly?

               (KELLY *moves away from* CLAUDETTE.)

CLAUDETTE   How about you? You itching to get married?
               Wear a posh frock and impress the relatives?

CELIA   Has your boyfriend popped the question yet?

               (LUCINDA *steps off the bench and crosses to*
               KELLY.)

LUCINDA   I didn't know you had a boyfriend.

CLAUDETTE   Have you? Have you got a boyfriend Kelly?

               (KELLY *shakes her head.*)

CLAUDETTE   Get out there girl. My Katy used to go up to
               the Tropicana. Come back full of it. You go up
               there?

               (KELLY *shakes her head.*)

CLAUDETTE   Bit of a raver on the quiet are we? Your
               mother lock you up, does she?

               (KELLY *shakes her head.*)

CLAUDETTE   Worried about her fun-seeking daughter with a
               rum and coke inside her.

KELLY   Don't think so. She's dead.

CELIA   ⎱ Oh dear.
CLAUDETTE   ⎰ Oh. Oh my . . .

               (SIOBHAN *enters in workout clothes carrying
               several skipping ropes, a box and some papers
               which she hands to* KELLY.)

SIOBHAN	Has anyone seen Rosie? Where's my special girl? Kelly. Here. Headache doesn't seem like much of an excuse to me but you can make yourself useful. Write each group member's name on the top of a form and then paper clip each one to a catalogue. She's late. She's never late.
CLAUDETTE	Probably canoodling with that Laurence somewhere.
SIOBHAN	Sincerely hope not.

(KELLY *takes the forms and catalogues from* SIOBHAN *and sits with them on the centre bench.*)

JEAN	What's all this . . .
LUCINDA	Catalogues?
SIOBHAN	Uh-Uh-Uh-Uh-Uh. Pleasure later. First the pain.

(SIOBHAN *hands out skipping ropes.*)

CLAUDETTE	Oh Lord.
LUCINDA	Thanks.
CELIA	Ah.
JEAN	Thank you.
SIOBHAN	Skipping burns up six hundred and thirty calories per hour.

(SIOBHAN *skips.*)

CELIA	Not doing it for an hour are we?
SIOBHAN	Cycling — two hundred and forty. Tennis — thirty eight calories an hour. Even jogging is only three hundred and thirty so look lively girls and follow me.

CELIA	Alright.
LUCINDA	OK.
JEAN	Off we go.

(SIOBHAN *skips out towards the hall.* CELIA, LUCINDA *and* JEAN *follow.*)

CLAUDETTE   Kelly. I'm sorry. If I went to a chiropodist he'd want to look in my mouth.

KELLY   They've started.

CLAUDETTE   You're about my Katy's age.

KELLY   I know.

CLAUDETTE   She's at university.

KELLY   I know. She went to my school.

CLAUDETTE   You were friends?

KELLY   She was clever.

CLAUDETTE   Who do you live with Kelly? Your dad? Brothers? Sisters? Who looks out for . . .

KELLY   I'll put the urn on.

CLAUDETTE   Tell me. Talk to me. Who do . . .

KELLY   LET GO OF ME.

(KELLY *heads towards the kitchen.* CLAUDETTE *picks up a hymn book.*)

CLAUDETTE   Must be hot in that jumper. Going to take it off for the weigh-in?

(KELLY *exits as* CELIA *enters from the hall, dragging her skipping rope behind her.* CLAUDETTE *throws the hymn book down.*)

CELIA   Siobhan requires your presence in the torture chamber.

CLAUDETTE   What? Oh. Bunking off, Celia?

CELIA   High impact. Bad for the joints. George would not approve.

CLAUDETTE	What about Mother Superior?
CELIA	Special dispensation. Relegated to catering duty.
CLAUDETTE	Wish I was. Here goes.

(CLAUDETTE *exits towards the hall.*)

CELIA	(*shouting after* CLAUDETTE) Get those knees up, woman.

(CELIA *heads towards the kitchen but stops as she sees* ROSIE *enter from the direction of the lavatories covered in confetti.*)

CELIA	Oh — I say. Rosie. How long have you been in there?
ROSIE	I was . . . I was watching the wedding from the gate and then I . . . Well I . . . I just . . .
CELIA	Decided to skip the skipping. Very wise. (*Shouting as she exits towards the kitchen.*) It looked like quite a do.

(ROSIE *sits, picking confetti off her clothes.*)

ROSIE	Was. Yes. Was. The bride was shining. Beautiful. And the groom was so proud. And they stood on the steps with just their fingertips touching. And they smiled. And the sun broke through the clouds.

(CELIA *enters from the kitchen.*)

CELIA	Kelly appears to be in control.
ROSIE	The sunlight reflected off the glass. Onto them. Like a halo. A halo of love. Happy. They were so happy.

(ROSIE *bursts into tears.*)

| CELIA | Rosie. I've cried at a few weddings myself but usually when I'm in some way connected. If spectating affects you so badly I'd think about finding another Saturday afternoon occupation. |

| ROSIE | What am I going to do? |

| CELIA | Do? Do about . . . |

| ROSIE | They've just whisked him away . . . |

| CELIA | What? Who? |

| ROSIE | There'll be an investigation . . . |

| CELIA | What? What are — |

| ROSIE | Laurence. Laurence. My Laurence. |

| CELIA | Why? What's he done, dear? |

| ROSIE | Nothing. And I know that Celia. He's very good at what he does. Full of life. Enthusiasm. And the children. All the children they love him. Trust him. And people can be very jealous. Very suspicious of that. |

| CELIA | Oh. Oh I see. Well — How . . . How awful. |

| ROSIE } | It's not true. |
| CELIA | You do realise those sort of allegations have to be . . . |

| ROSIE } | But it's all a disgusting lie. |
| CELIA | Rosie. |

| ROSIE } | Laurence is good and kind. |
| CELIA | Rosie. |

| ROSIE | And I love him. I love him. I love him. |

(ROSIE *bursts into tears again.*)

| CELIA | Exactly. Rosie dear. We all have different faces. I'm jolly with the milkman. Stern with |

the gardener and placid with Ted. I shout at
the lady who pays my pension because she's
slow and I whisper to the doctor because he's
charming. And as for those we love. We look
for the face that we want to see. And we give
them the face that pleases the most. Love is
blind, dear. Trust to the eyesight of others.
I'm sure he'll get a fair hearing.

ROSIE   Like the one you just gave him.

CELIA   People aren't just spirited away for no reason.
             There must be some evidence.

ROSIE   Letters, that's all. Anonymous letters. That's
             not evidence, it's spite. And I'll never believe
             it. Never.

             (SIOBHAN *enters followed by* LUCINDA,
             CLAUDETTE *and* JEAN, *trailing their skipping
             ropes.*)

SIOBHAN   I think we've earned our tea, ladies. Rosie
             poppet — what's wrong?

ROSIE   Nothing. Touch of hay fever.

LUCINDA   Been sniffing those wedding bouquets again?

SIOBHAN   Always the bridesmaid, yes?

ROSIE   Yes. Always the bridesmaid. I'll set out the
             chairs.

             (ROSIE *exits tearfully into the hall.*)

SIOBHAN   Sweetheart what's the . . . (*Shouting towards
             the hall.*) I'm talking to you — Rosie . . .

CLAUDETTE   You missed a treat, Celia. I'm a lean mean
             exercise machine. I nearly broke the record.

LUCINDA   For falling over or moaning.

CLAUDETTE	Cheeky.
SIOBHAN	Where's Kelly? Do I have to do everything myself?

(CLAUDETTE *and* LUCINDA *exit into the kitchen*.)

CELIA   That's the burden of power, Siobhan.

(CELIA *exits into the kitchen*.)

SIOBHAN   (*shouting towards the kitchen*) Bring me out a herbal. What's wrong with Rosie?

JEAN   I . . . I — don't know I . . .

SIOBHAN   This place is a pig sty. A pig sty.

JEAN   Yes. Yes I'll . . .

(JEAN *clears up,* SIOBHAN *tidies the centre bench and sorts through the catalogues and forms*.)

SIOBHAN   Leave that. And give me a hand with these. The confessional's open. What is it this time? I'm all ears.

(JEAN *helps* SIOBHAN *with the catalogues and forms*.)

JEAN   I've had a stressful week. Very — very stressful.

SIOBHAN   And have we put any on?

JEAN   Possibly.

SIOBHAN   Realisation. You have to stick to the maintenance plan. Getting there is half the battle, Jean. It's staying there that sorts the women from the girls.

(SIOBHAN *finds cash box in her locker and turns her back on* JEAN. JEAN *clips forms to catalogues nervously*.)

JEAN	I know . . . it's just — new shoes for the kids. Tax for the car. We're a bit short this month. Fifty pounds short to be precise . . . Siobhan we need that money we . . .

(SIOBHAN *returns to the bench clutching the cash box.*)

SIOBHAN	You're telling me fifty pounds is the difference between happy and sad.
JEAN	No. Between hot and cold. It's for the gas bill.
SIOBHAN	Take another job then.
JEAN	I'm doing five as it is.
SIOBHAN	Gregory earns good money.
JEAN	Yes. But he says I should put more in. To the household. If you — if I insist on working all hours. I'm sorry Siobhan but he told me to ask for —
SIOBHAN	Oh I see. That's what it's really about. He can't bear you being independent.
JEAN	I can't do this. Too fiddly. I'm shaking. I'm . . .

(JEAN *throws the catalogues down.*)

SIOBHAN	I smell a crisis. Spit it out.
JEAN	Gregory, he . . .
SIOBHAN	Look at me.
JEAN	Gregory wants me to get my money back because he wants me to . . .
SIOBHAN	Yes?
JEAN	Gregory wants me to leave the group.

(*A silence.*)

SIOBHAN	HOW DARE HE.
JEAN	Please don't be angry with me.
SIOBHAN	Don't do this to me, Jean. Not today. I have enough worries.

JEAN   I'm sorry but he . . .

SIOBHAN   Why?

JEAN   It does cost . . . and . . .

SIOBHAN   And?

JEAN   He says I've lost the weight and he doesn't understand why I have to keep coming here.

SIOBHAN   Moron. And?

JEAN   He thinks it may not be good for me. The lifeplan. My work goals. He wants me at home with him. He wants me . . .

SIOBHAN   He wants you on a leash Jean, that's what he wants.

JEAN   He says I'm obsessed and . . .

SIOBHAN   What does he know?

JEAN   He is my husband.

SIOBHAN   He's a control freak and he gets a kick out of playing with your head. For God's sake, that's why you came to me in the first place.

JEAN   Please don't shout. Yes I had a few problems and . . .

SIOBHAN   YOU WERE IN DESPAIR, THANK YOU. Let's not shilly-shally Jean, you were practically a basket case. That man led you such a dance you didn't know what day of the week it was. Pills. Therapy. YOU WERE A WRECK SWEETHEART, YES?

JEAN	I'd lost a little confidence.
SIOBHAN	AND MOST OF YOUR MARBLES.
JEAN	Sssh. Please.
SIOBHAN	And who picked you up? Who put you back together again?
JEAN	I . . . I . . . I don't know what to do. I don't . . . all I know is that Gregory wants me to leave.
SIOBHAN	See your lover again.
JEAN	I can't.
SIOBHAN	You can. And you must. He made you smile, Jean.
JEAN	But Gregory, he . . .
SIOBHAN	You can't let Gregory stand between you and salvation.
JEAN	No. Yes. No. Oh, I don't know what to do. I don't know . . .
SIOBHAN	Secrets. The power lies in secrets, Jean. Think long and hard about secrets and you'll come to your own decision. OK?
JEAN	OK.

(CLAUDETTE *enters with* SIOBHAN'S *tea.* LUCINDA *follows.*)

CLAUDETTE	Here we are. One cup of zero calorie beverage.
SIOBHAN	Where's Rosie?
LUCINDA	What's next? Aerobics. Gymnastics.

(CELIA *enters.*)

CELIA	Potholing?

SIOBHAN   (*shouts towards the hall*) ROSIE I NEED YOU
               . . . Finish up your tea and while we're in here
               — Jean. Hand around the catalogues.

               (ROSIE *enters and sits.* JEAN *hands out the
               catalogues.*)

SIOBHAN   You missed register, sweetheart. Not like you.

               (KELLY *enters from the kitchen.*)

LUCINDA   So what's all this about . . .

               (SIOBHAN *picks up a catalogue.*)

SIOBHAN   The new Slim for Life winter season
               catalogue. I don't hold with much that comes
               out of head office but this is a treat. Top
               designs for the larger lady. I want you all to
               select the outfit of your choice.

CELIA   Lovely clothes Siobhan, but I can't afford
               seventy pounds for a 'love-handle concealing
               floral blouse'.

LUCINDA   A hundred and twenty pounds for a 'hip-
               skirting blazer'.

JEAN   As for the underwear . . .

SIOBHAN   Ladies. Order through me and there's an
               immediate forty per cent discount. And you
               can pay on terms. Plus it's fourteen days
               approval. No obligation.

JEAN   There are some beautiful clothes in here.

SIOBHAN   (*flicking through a catalogue and indicating
               to* JEAN) Evening wear. That dress. That
               scarlet dress. Perfect for a rendezvous, don't
               you think?

JEAN   Yes. Maybe. Perhaps. I . . .

SIOBHAN   Lucinda — outfit for that interview. Claudette
                 — a little something to impress the dons.
                 Celia — some very fetching walking boots at
                 the back here. And Rosie. Find something for
                 yourself. That pleases you. To cheer you up,
                 yes? Aside from that could we all invest in a
                 party outfit? I want us all to dress up for our
                 Christmas meeting.

CELIA   ⎱   What a nice idea.
CLAUDETTE   ⎰   Why not?

SIOBHAN   Let's make it a night to remember. Have a bit
                 of a buffet — low calorie of course. Make it a
                 celebration of all we've achieved here. And
                 further to that . . .

                 (SIOBHAN *holds up a sponsor form.*)

SIOBHAN   Sponsor forms.

LUCINDA   ⎱   Oh no.
CLAUDETTE   ⎰

CELIA   ⎱   Ah.
JEAN   ⎰   What are we . . .

LUCINDA   You mean we have to ask people for money?

CELIA   Not very good at that. Once did door to door
                 for Help the Aged and ended up putting my
                 pension in the box to save myself the
                 embarrassment.

SIOBHAN   I've written what I want you to say at the top
                 here . . . Hello I am Lucinda — Celia —
                 whatever — I am engaged on a programme of
                 self-improvement, would you like to help me
                 to achieve my goal and donate to charity at the
                 same time?

LUCINDA   You've written us a script.

SIOBHAN   Not just a pretty face.

LUCINDA   Well aware of that. Just as well. Otherwise I'd
             be inclined to go up to people and say excuse
             me I'm as big as a bus but if you give me fifty
             pence I might shift a few pounds.

             (*All laugh.*)

SIOBHAN   Humour is a very cheap defence mechanism,
             Lucinda.

LUCINDA   Why don't you invest in some then?

             (*A silence.*)

LUCINDA   Oh come on. Lighten up everybody. It was a . . .

SIOBHAN   You want to get to the top you need to be in
             control. And you're not poppet, are you? You
             are not in control.

LUCINDA   Which charity?

SIOBHAN   We'll decide whenever. OK. Everybody up.
             You have one month. Get those sponsors. Lose
             that weight. Finish the year with a bang. Time
             for the weigh-in. Go, go, go — DAY BY DAY
             BY DAY . . .

ALL   The pounds are falling away.

             (CLAUDETTE, LUCINDA, CELIA, JEAN *and* KELLY
             exit. ROSIE *peels off her outer clothes.*)

SIOBHAN   Rosie. What's the . . .

ROSIE   Don't want to talk about it.

SIOBHAN   OK. Here.

             (SIOBHAN *hands* ROSIE *a tissue.*)

ROSIE   Thanks.

SIOBHAN   Whatever it is I'm here for you. Come round
             tonight. Empty house. I'm no good in an
             empty house.

ROSIE   I . . . I think I've lost weight.

SIOBHAN   Excellent news.

ROSIE   Yes. Lost weight this week. No marshmallows.
               No liquorice wheels. No love hearts . . . Help
               me. Help me please.

               (ROSIE *bursts into tears.* SIOBHAN *embraces
               her.*)

SIOBHAN   Sacrifice. Sweet sweet sacrifice.

               (*Blackout.*)

                        Scene Three

Christmas.

*The same. The sound of 'Ding Dong Merrily On High' being
played on the organ in the adjacent church.* CELIA *stands
huddled in her coat by the heater.* SIOBHAN, *in her new outfit,
hoovers the rug beside the centre bench.*

CELIA   Is that strictly necessary?

SIOBHAN   What?

               (LUCINDA *enters wearing Rudolf antlers.*)

CELIA   ⎫   I said do we . . .
LUCINDA   ⎭   Hello everybody.

SIOBHAN   I CAN'T HEAR YOU.

               (LUCINDA *exits.*)

CELIA   I SAID DO WE REALLY NEED TO . . .

               (*The vacuum cleaner stops droning suddenly.*)

CELIA   HOOVER THAT TATTY RUG.

SIOBHAN   Yes we do. If we have to be in here we might
               as well make it comfortable.

               (LUCINDA *enters with the plug in her hand. She
               gives it to* SIOBHAN.)

LUCINDA   So where are the cocktails? Where's the jazz
               band? The male stripper?

SIOBHAN   This is not a party, Lucinda. It's a meeting.
               OK? A meeting. And take those things off.
               You look ridiculous.

               (SIOBHAN *exits towards the hall with the
               vacuum cleaner.* LUCINDA *removes her
               antlers.*)

LUCINDA   And a happy Christmas to you too. What are
               the Brownies doing in the hall?

CELIA   I'm not sure. But I do know Siobhan isn't a
               women to be crossed tonight.

LUCINDA   Is she ever?

CELIA   Had a nasty contretemps with the Vicar. She
               was screaming 'Christian charity' and had to
               be dragged from the hall. He's given her the
               changing room as a favour.

LUCINDA   Some favour.

CELIA   Oh it is — a huge favour as far as this church
               is concerned, believe me. On a par with
               handing over the keys to paradise.

LUCINDA   What do you think. Da-da!

               (LUCINDA *takes off her coat to reveal her
               dress.*)

LUCINDA   Exclusive Slim for Life fashion. 'Especially
               flattering for those with heavy hips'.

CELIA   Oh it is. Very flattering. Very flattering indeed.

LUCINDA   Thanks.

CELIA   Not that flattering.

LUCINDA   Well?

CELIA   Oh. Yes.

            (CELIA *takes off her coat.*)

LUCINDA   Lovely. Very seasonal.

CELIA   The slashed V-neck is supposed to slim you down.

LUCINDA   It does.

CELIA   I don't look like Mary Queen of Scots after a bad swing?

LUCINDA   You look fantastic. Wish I did.

            (LUCINDA *looks in the mirror and applies make-up.* CELIA *returns to the heater.*)

CELIA   You do.

LUCINDA   I've just been to the office party, Celia. Very boozy.

CELIA   Oh dear.

LUCINDA   I did my best to flirt with the man who controls my destiny.

CELIA   Very wise.

LUCINDA   But he kept forgetting my name.

CELIA   Ah. Well. Can happen to anyone.

LUCINDA   It was written on a badge on my chest. My hip flattering design got me nowhere. To him I'm just a nameless girl with a big bum.

CELIA

You're Lucinda. You're jolly nice and you're five pounds off target. Stop feeling sorry for yourself and have a reduced calorie sausage roll.

(CELIA *opens a box that lies on the bench.* LUCINDA *takes a sausage roll and eats.*)

CELIA

I cooked a big batch. George is coming over. For the duration. We're going to plan our route. Keep him company, too. Must be hard. This time of year. If you're on your own.

LUCINDA

Yes. It is.

CELIA

No family. Not going.

LUCINDA

Never look back. That's what Siobhan says isn't it? Never look back.

CELIA

She does, yes. But a sense of perspective never did anyone any harm. If you ask me.

LUCINDA

Celia. I had three gins at the party and I didn't use Slimline tonic.

CELIA

There's half a pound of butter in these and I used the last of the lo-sodium salt to de-ice the driveway. Be a devil. It's Christmas.

(CELIA *passes the box to* LUCINDA.)

LUCINDA

And it's only three weeks 'til my interview. I can't. Mustn't.

(CLAUDETTE *enters in her coat.*)

CLAUDETTE

Hold on to your hats girls, here comes trouble!

LUCINDA
CELIA   }
CLAUDETTE

Claudette.
Hello.
Are you ready for my super-slinky ultra sexy Slim For Life transformation?

CELIA	Oh yes.
LUCINDA	Let's see it then.
CLAUDETTE	Lock up your sons. Claudette is in town.

(CLAUDETTE *takes off her coat to reveal an outrageously short mini-skirt and revealing top.* SIOBHAN *enters.*)

CELIA	Oh I say.
LUCINDA	Amazing.
SIOBHAN	Celia did you have some — what the hell are you wearing?

CLAUDETTE   It's all from the catalogue.

SIOBHAN   Yes. The 'Teen Dream' section. Sorry sweetheart, but your mini-skirt days are long gone. And what's going on? Give them to me. Give them to me. This minute.

(CLAUDETTE *picks up the sausage rolls.*)

CLAUDETTE   What's a sausage roll Siobhan?

SIOBHAN   Cyanide in a pastry case as far as you're concerned. Hand them over.

CLAUDETTE   I thought we were celebrating.

SIOBHAN   Celebrating, not back-tracking.

CLAUDETTE   I've lost a stone and a half in total. I deserve a treat. I've done well.

(CLAUDETTE *eats a sausage roll.*)

SIOBHAN   Oh yes you've done well. Very well. So well that your daughter isn't coming home for Christmas.

LUCINDA	What?
CELIA	Oh I . . .

SIOBHAN   So well that she wishes you'd never visited. So well that she had to tell her friends you were the college cleaner. Have a couple more why don't you? Best that I'm in charge of the food, don't you think?

(SIOBHAN *picks up the sausage rolls and exits into the kitchen.* CLAUDETTE *slumps on to a bench.*)

CLAUDETTE I've bought a little pudding for one. And I've stocked up on mince pies and soppy videos. It's Christmas. And if Siobhan thinks I'm going to spend it in purgatory she's . . .

(ROSIE *enters in her coat, carrying a bowl in a carrier bag.*)

ROSIE Been ousted by the Brownies have we?

CELIA Hello dear.

LUCINDA Surprise us then, Rosie.

CLAUDETTE Yes. Let's have a look.

ROSIE Just a salad nicoise without the eggs or the fish in an oil-free dress . . .

LUCINDA No Rosie. You.

ROSIE Me?

CELIA What lurks beneath the coat?

ROSIE A multitude of sins.

CLAUDETTE Let's see.

ROSIE I'm scared. Where's Siobhan?

LUCINDA Out there. Come on.

(ROSIE *puts the bowl down and takes her coat off slowly.*)

ROSIE	Alright. Alright, but . . .
CLAUDETTE	Very nice.
CELIA	Very fetching.

ROSIE   Yes, but I can't get the button done up at the back.

CELIA   Let me see.

CLAUDETTE   Has your Laurence been force-feeding you eclairs again?

LUCINDA	Claudette.
CELIA	Oh really.

CLAUDETTE   Sorry. Sorry. I forgot.

ROSIE	Lucky you.
CELIA	Pass me my bag.

(CLAUDETTE *passes* CELIA *her handbag.* CELIA *finds sewing kit and moves button on the back of* ROSIE'S *skirt.*)

CLAUDETTE   Any news? I mean have they decided if . . .

LUCINDA   Don't.

ROSIE   Just Mummy and me for Christmas. Like it's always been. Like it always will be. She's not terribly well. So — Florence Nightingale time for me. Lady with the lamp.

(SIOBHAN *enters from the kitchen wearing rubber gloves carrying a bin liner.*)

SIOBHAN   Disgrace.

LUCINDA   Here comes the fire extinguisher.

SIOBHAN   That kitchen is a disgrace. Oh Rosie, poppet — what are you doing?

ROSIE   Nothing.

SIOBHAN   Did you bring the salad? Lucinda, pick up all
                   that rubbish.

                   (SIOBHAN *hands bin liner to* LUCINDA *and exits
                   towards the hall.*)

ROSIE   }   Quickly Celia.
LUCINDA   Yes Siobhan. No Siobhan. Three bags full
                   Siobhan. Do you think she's like this at home?

CLAUDETTE   (*looking out towards the hall*) Jean's here.

LUCINDA   How does her husband cope?

ROSIE   I don't think he does. I mean — well poor
                  Siobhan, she's . . .

CLAUDETTE   She's what?

                  (SIOBHAN *enters from the hall and takes the bin
                  liner from* LUCINDA.)

SIOBHAN   Finished? Rosie, what's going on?

ROSIE   Nothing. Nothing at all.

SIOBHAN   That outfit's on approval. Don't think you'll
                  get your money back if it's been mucked about
                  with.

LUCINDA   It's too small.

ROSIE   No — no, it . . .

CLAUDETTE   (*to* LUCINDA) Shut up.

SIOBHAN   It's a fourteen. I ordered you a fourteen. Let
                  me . . .

                  (SIOBHAN *looks at the back of* ROSIE'S *skirt.*)

ROSIE   I am a fourteen. That's my size. Fourteen. I
                  should be a fourteen. I mean I was a fourteen.
                  Once.

SIOBHAN	I was once an age one to two — that doesn't mean I'm going to squeeze myself into a romper suit, does it? Well does it?
ROSIE	Siobhan please, I . . .
SIOBHAN	Later. Not now. Not now.

(SIOBHAN *scoops up the salad and exits towards the kitchen.*)

ROSIE	(*shouting towards the kitchen*) I'm sorry, I'm sorry I'm . . .
CLAUDETTE	What is eating her tonight?
LUCINDA	Me if she doesn't get a move on. I'm starving.

(JEAN *enters wheeling a dressmaker's mannequin with food wrappers attached.*)

JEAN	Siobhan. Siobhan. Where do you want me to . . . Oh hello, where's she . . .
CELIA	Oh, not sin-bags.

CELIA	Not tonight.
CLAUDETTE	Oh, here it comes.
LUCINDA	Oh no.

JEAN	Sin-bags it is, I'm afraid. Siobhan says it's to be a meeting as per. I'll pop it over here.
CELIA	There you are Rosie. All done.
JEAN	What do you think?

(JEAN *takes off her coat.*)

CLAUDETTE	Smashing.
CELIA	Wonderful.
ROSIE	Lovely.
LUCINDA	Very nice.

(SIOBHAN *enters with a tray of glasses and two bottles of 'Lo-Fizz'.*)

SIOBHAN	Lucinda. Bring the scales in, will you?
LUCINDA	Stick a broom up my . . .
SIOBHAN	Spare me the verbals. Just do it. Jean. That's not the dress I chose for you.

(LUCINDA *exits towards the hall*.)

JEAN	No. It wasn't practical.
SIOBHAN	Wasn't meant to be.
JEAN	But this outfit will travel well. Gregory and I are going away for Christmas. Just the two of us.
SIOBHAN	What?
JEAN	Yes — oh yes — we had it all out the other night and . . .
SIOBHAN	I do hope you know what you're doing.
CLAUDETTE	She's over twenty one.
JEAN	No — Siobhan's just worried. As a friend. Because I told her all about my affair and she . . .
CLAUDETTE CELIA ROSIE	What? Oh Jean. Affair! Gosh . . .
JEAN	Was wonderful. I've made a decision. On my own.
SIOBHAN	You've done what?
JEAN	You made me realise that secrets just aren't healthy. Too powerful. Too . . .
SIOBHAN	No. No, that's not what I . . .

| JEAN | So Gregory and I have told each other everything. Bless you Siobhan. You were right. |

SIOBHAN   Here. Here.

(SIOBHAN *pours 'Lo-Fizz' into glasses.* LUCINDA *enters with bathroom scales and sets them down.*)

LUCINDA   The Brownies are doing a nativity play. Problems — no one wants to be Joseph.

SIOBHAN   Lo-Fizz. Have some Lo-Fizz, shall we? Latest product from Slim For Life. Negative food value. Oldie Worldie farmhouse recipe.

LUCINDA   } You're spilling it. Here.
CLAUDETTE } Oh I bet, yeah.

(LUCINDA *helps* SIOBHAN.)

SIOBHAN   Lots of lovely rurally herby things.

JEAN   In fact I've been thinking. Now I've cleared the air . . .

CLAUDETTE Cheers everybody.

JEAN   I'll definitely leave the group in the New Year.

ALL   Cheers.

SIOBHAN   You can't.

JEAN   Oh but I can Siobhan, don't you see? Because it's my choice. Not Gregory's. All mine. And you helped me to do that. Thank you.

(KELLY *enters in coat.*)

KELLY   I'm sorry, I'm sorry — I'm sorry, I'm . . .

SIOBHAN   Kelly. Thank God you're here.

CLAUDETTE	Oh hello. Didn't see you . . .
LUCINDA	Hi Kelly.
CELIA	Hello dear.
ROSIE	Kelly.
SIOBHAN	Come on. You can help with the food. I said come on. Move.

(SIOBHAN *grabs* KELLY *and they exit towards the kitchen.*)

CLAUDETTE   Hey — I don't like the way she bosses her around.

LUCINDA   She bosses us all around. Haven't you noticed?

CLAUDETTE   It's just beginning to dawn on me.

ROSIE   There's definitely a hint of something rustic in this.

CLAUDETTE   Um. Fertiliser. Oh for a Malibu and coke.

(*The sound of a carol being sung by the Brownies in the adjacent hall.*)

JEAN   Ah. Sweet.

LUCINDA	Yeah.
CLAUDETTE	Yes.

(LUCINDA *looks out towards the hall.*)

JEAN   I'll miss the kids. We've sent them to their cousin's.

CLAUDETTE   You won't miss them at all. No computer games. No Sound of Music and no tempting chocolate selection packs.

ROSIE   Oh don't. Hungry.

JEAN   That s very true. Children can make you fat.

LUCINDA   So can parents. Parents can make you fat.

CLAUDETTE   What?

LUCINDA   I've been thinking. Thinking about coming
             here. Trying to lose weight. Always trying to
             lose weight and, well . . . I know now. I know
             where it all comes from.

CLAUDETTE   I hope you consulted the oracle of love, life
             and calorie control.

LUCINDA   No. I don't need Siobhan.

CELIA   Blasphemy.

LUCINDA   I've worked it all out. For myself. See. See
             when I was six, I was in love. I was in love
             with a womble.

ROSIE   Which one?

LUCINDA   Uncle Bulgaria.

CLAUDETTE   Have I missed something?

CELIA   Three gins and an office party, dear.

LUCINDA   I had the soft toy. Dad brought him back from
             a business trip. Took my womble everywhere
             with me. Eventually his waistcoat was matted
             with toothpaste and his nose was hanging on
             by a thread but I wouldn't give him up. And
             then one day my mother . . . flipped. I'd
             wandered into the kitchen. Marital minefield.
             Looked like a smash-the-crockery stall. Wrong
             place. Wrong time. She grabbed Uncle
             Bulgaria, cut his head off with the meat
             cleaver and stuffed him down the waste
             disposal. I climbed on to the draining board
             and saw his paws sticking up out of the hole
             covered in a film of spinach. And I howled.

             (SIOBHAN *enters with a tray of food.* LUCINDA
             notices her.)

LUCINDA   And then my dad. Fag in hand. Thrust
                Smarties down my throat in between sobs. And
                it worked. It shut me up.

                (*A silence.*)

LUCINDA   Realisation, Siobhan.

SIOBHAN   That's not realisation, it's navel
                contemplation and it gets you nowhere. Ask
                Jean. She's spent years staring into her own
                head and look where it's taken her. Right back
                where she started from.

                (KELLY *enters with a tray of plates.*)

JEAN   That's not true, I . . .

SIOBHAN   Three hundred and fifty calories per plate. We
                have a portion of salad . . .

CLAUDETTE   I'll do that, Kelly. You sit down. Take your
                coat off.

                (CLAUDETTE *takes tray from* KELLY *who sits but
                doesn't take her coat off.*)

SIOBHAN   One ounce of low-fat crisps.

CLAUDETTE   Don't eat them all at once, girls.

SIOBHAN   One stuffed mushroom.

CLAUDETTE   A whole one?

SIOBHAN   Sliced pepper. And two of Celia's reduced fat
                sausage rolls which taste surprisingly buttery.

LUCINDA   (*winking at* CELIA) Well done, Celia.

SIOBHAN   Happy Christmas to you all. There is no need
                for the festive season to interfere with the
                lifeplan. If you do happen to overdo it,
                remember to . . .

| ALL | } | Compensate. |
| KELLY | | Compensate. Compensate. Compensate. |

SIOBHAN   Yes. You have a splurge. A moment of madness. I've done it myself . . .

CLAUDETTE   There's an admission.

SIOBHAN   You reduce your intake the following day. Get into the habit of doing so. And eventually once you hit target you'll be able to . . .

| ALL | } | Maintain. |
| KELLY | | Maintain. Maintain. Maintain. |

SIOBHAN   Yes.

KELLY   Maintain. Main . . .

SIOBHAN   Thank you Kelly. Yes. This meeting is open.

(SIOBHAN *picks up her handbell and rings it.*)

SIOBHAN   Not slim for today . . . Not slim for tomorrow, but . . .

| ALL | } | Slim for life. |
| LUCINDA | | Slim for life. Great salad Rosie. |

| ROSIE | } | Thanks. |
| SIOBHAN | | Claudette. Read this week's mantra, please. |

(SIOBHAN *holds out book for* CLAUDETTE.)

CLAUDETTE   I'm eating.

SIOBHAN   Do you good to come up for air. Come on.

(CLAUDETTE *takes the book.*)

CLAUDETTE   'Never let a man stand between you and a virtually fat-free diet. Love is a summer of pleasure. A perfect body is a lifetime of joy.'

SIOBHAN   Second that Rosie, yes?

(CLAUDETTE *hands the book back to* SIOBHAN.)

CLAUDETTE   I'll take the summer of pleasure.

LUCINDA   Weekend'd do me.

SIOBHAN   Do you mind?

(SIOBHAN *rings her handbell.*)

SIOBHAN   Agenda. Sin-bags and weigh-in. First, though
             — I totted up the sponsor money and we have
             raised the grand total of one hundred and
             seventy five pounds. Give ourselves a clap,
             shall we?

(*All clap lamely.*)

LUCINDA   So where is this hundred and seventy five pounds?

SIOBHAN   In the bank, where'd you think?

LUCINDA   Why is it still in the bank?

SIOBHAN   Any further thoughts on a charity?

CELIA   ⎫ Blind society.
CLAUDETTE   ⎬ That Africa thing.
JEAN   ⎭ Cancer Research.

SIOBHAN   That's why Lucinda, OK?

LUCINDA   Sure you haven't been dipping into the till,
             Siobhan?

SIOBHAN   I beg your pardon.

LUCINDA   Stranger things have happened. Not many
             members. Lean times.

SIOBHAN   I have never been so insulted in my life!

LUCINDA   I'm only joking, for . . .

SIOBHAN   As if. As if I could possibly . . . I drive an
             estate car, thank you. I live in a three bed
             detached and this is a twenty one carat
             solitaire. I am very very comfortable.

ROSIE   Oh but you're not Siobhan, you poor thing. You're not.

SIOBHAN   Shut up Rosie.

ROSIE   Comfortable at . . .

SIOBHAN   Sin-bags.

ROSIE   But you told me . . .

SIOBHAN   SIN-BAGS.

ROSIE   Things must be very hard indeed, now Simon's left you.

                  (*A silence.*)

SIOBHAN   Remind me never to call you as a character witness, poppet. Here. Bank book. Satisfied?

                  (*She finds building society book in her handbag and hands it to* LUCINDA.)

LUCINDA   Look, I'm sorry. Sorry, I didn't mean anything, I . . .

CELIA   Is it true dear? About Simon? Maybe we could be of some help?

SIOBHAN   Of course it isn't true and don't patronise me Celia, I'm here to help you. Rosie has a very loose grip on reality and a sugar-jaded brain, haven't you sweetheart?

ROSIE   But you said he —

SIOBHAN   You silly, silly girl. I was speaking metaphorically.

ROSIE   Were you?

SIOBHAN   It was a 'what if' scenario. To make you realise how easy it is to cope without a man. OK? Remember now?

ROSIE	I'm confused, I . . .
SIOBHAN	I know you are poppet. That's why I'm here — Kelly. Sin-bags. Move. Come on.

(KELLY *wheels the mannequin forward. All find their carrier bags containing wrappers.* SIOBHAN *hands drawing pins to* KELLY. SIOBHAN *rings her bell.*)

SIOBHAN	After me. There's no sin . . .
ALL	Like a food sin.
SIOBHAN	Celia?
CELIA	One bag of iced gems and a packet of Garibaldis. A few attacks of the nibbles.
SIOBHAN	What have I told you time and time again? You keep a tupperware box in the fridge full of chopped raw vegetables.
CLAUDETTE	Yum yum.
SIOBHAN	Dried apricots in the larder. Bramleys in your bedside table. Sugar-free gum in your pocket. The right food, Celia. Prepared in advance. Be prepared, alright?
CLAUDETTE	Dib dob dib.
SIOBHAN	Will you shut up Claudette.
CLAUDETTE } SIOBHAN	Charming. Jean.

(JEAN *hands wrappers to* KELLY.)

JEAN	One packet of peanuts.
SIOBHAN	Nuts may be très Linda McCartney but they're full of fat.
JEAN	One tiny packet of peanuts?

SIOBHAN	Give it six months of Gregory and it'll be a plantation, sweetheart. Claudette. Hurry up Kelly.

(CLAUDETTE *hands cake box to* KELLY.)

SIOBHAN	Well. Well. Well. Been at the cream cakes again have we?
CLAUDETTE	Only bite-size. Miniature.
SIOBHAN	Unlike you.
LUCINDA CLAUDETTE SIOBHAN	} Hey! Just a minute. Sit down. Rosie. Rosie. I'm waiting.
ROSIE	I . . . I'd rather not.
SIOBHAN	You'd rather not. Oh fine — fine. Liberty hall. Free and easy. Your choice.
ROSIE	Thank you.
SIOBHAN	You just wait 'til the weigh-in young lady. Lucinda.
LUCINDA	Nothing to declare.
SIOBHAN	No sins?
LUCINDA	Plenty. But you can't stick a drawing pin through a glass bottle. Rice cakes and alcohol. May not be out of the Slim for Life Bible, but I've lost four pounds. I've confessed, let's leave it at that.
SIOBHAN	No. No let's not leave it at that. You call me. You call me if you're tempted.
LUCINDA	I've had no time, I — it was just a bad week.
SIOBHAN	We don't have bad weeks here.

CLAUDETTE	Leave her alone Siobhan. She's under pressure.
SIOBHAN	Who isn't under pressure?
CLAUDETTE	She's got her interview shortly.
SIOBHAN	And she's not going to get that job looking like a washed-up old lush is she . . . Kelly — get your wrappers out. Now.
LUCINDA	Thanks a lot.

(KELLY *finds her wrappers, boxes and labels and fixes them to the mannequin.*)

CLAUDETTE	You're very lifelike, Siobhan. For a robot.
SIOBHAN KELLY LUCINDA	Sticks and stones. Four Dundee cakes. Leave it Claudette.
CLAUDETTE	You may be a size eight but that's about all you have going for you.
SIOBHAN KELLY	Damn sight more than you, sweetheart. Five boxes of Maltesers.
CELIA JEAN KELLY	Now let's not . . . This isn't . . . Sugar. Bags of . . .
CLAUDETTE	I am going to go all out this Christmas, Siobhan. Brandy snaps. Clotted cream . . .
SIOBHAN LUCINDA JEAN KELLY CLAUDETTE	Oh are you . . . Leave it. I think . . . And condensed milk. Five tins. Half a turkey. Cranberry sauce. Plum pudding . . .

(KELLY *returns to her seat.*)

CLAUDETTE   And then, Siobhan. Then I am going to bake a
              huge cake with chocolate and butter cream and
              pipe your name in big letters on the top and
              eat the bloody thing whole.

SIOBHAN   You do that, sweetheart. And come New Year
              when you're stuffed stupid and hate yourself
              don't come running to me.

CLAUDETTE   I don't hate myself.

SIOBHAN   OF COURSE YOU HATE YOURSELF, YOU
              ALL HATE YOURSELVES, YOU'RE . . .
              YOU'RE FAT FAT FAT FAT FAT FAT. That
              what you want, is it? You — you're fat. You
              — you're fat and you poppet are definitely no
              doubt about it fat. In here you are improving
              yourselves, yes? Out there you are all plain
              fat. Fat. Fat. Fat. And to be frank, right now
              you disgust me — OK? Happy? That what you
              want? NOW CAN WE GET ON WITH THIS
              MEETING. Weigh-in. Weigh-in. Weigh-in.

              (SIOBHAN *rings her bell manically.*)

SIOBHAN   Rosie. Move. Now.

ROSIE   Siobhan. I'm sorry, I think I . . .

SIOBHAN   JUST PUT IT ON THE SCALES FATTY.

LUCINDA   ⎫ What?
CLAUDETTE   ⎬ You can't . . .
CELIA   ⎪ That's hardly the . . .
JEAN   ⎭ Siobhan.

              (ROSIE *takes off her shoes and steps on to the
              scales.* SIOBHAN *reads the gauge.*)

SIOBHAN   You have gained three pounds this week,
              Rosie. Three pounds.

ROSIE   I know, I . . .

SIOBHAN   Three pounds.

ROSIE	Oh dear.
SIOBHAN	How many hours have I put into you? How many phone calls? How many visits?
CLAUDETTE	Leave her alone.
ROSIE	I'm sorry. I'm sorry, I . . . I just felt lonely and I . . .
SIOBHAN	Lonely. LONELY — YOU HAVE ME.
ROSIE	But I miss Laurence and I . . .
SIOBHAN	Laurence? LAURENCE WAS MAKING YOU FAT.
CLAUDETTE	Siobhan.
ROSIE	Yes, but now he's gone and I . . .
SIOBHAN	FOR GOD'S SAKE THAT'S WHY I GOT RID OF HIM FOR YOU.

(*A silence.*)

ROSIE	What?
CELIA	Oh my good Lord.
SIOBHAN	No, I mean I . . . just a . . .
ROSIE	What? You . . . You . . .
CELIA	The letters. You wrote the letters.
SIOBHAN	I . . .
ROSIE	It was you. It was you . . . Oh my . . .
SIOBHAN	Rosie. Sweetheart.
ROSIE	NO. NO. NO.

(ROSIE *runs into the hall.*)

SIOBHAN	Wait, I . . . Who's next? Who's next . . .

(SIOBHAN *rings her bell.*)

SIOBHAN	Come on. Come on. After me. After me girls. The more pounds I lose — yes? Come on. I said the more pounds I lose. AFTER ME. The more pounds I lose . . .

(*A silence.*)

KELLY	The more life I gain.
CLAUDETTE	No Kelly. Kelly, don't.

(KELLY *walks towards* SIOBHAN.)

KELLY	The more pounds I lose the more life I gain.
SIOBHAN	You must be close to target.
KELLY	The more pounds . . .
SIOBHAN	Got my bell ready. Is it going to ring for you?
KELLY	I lose the more life I gain . . .
SIOBHAN	Take your coat off, good girl. Commitment. Discipline. Sacrifice. Realisation and salvation . . .

(KELLY *takes off her coat. She wears very few clothes and is very thin. She steps on to the scales.* SIOBHAN *stands directly in front of her.*)

SIOBHAN	Salvation for you, Kelly.

CLAUDETTE	Oh my . . .
LUCINDA	What on . . .
CELIA	Oh God . . .
JEAN	For pity's . . .
SIOBHAN	Salvation.

KELLY	THE MORE POUNDS I LOSE THE MORE LIFE I GAIN.
SIOBHAN	Salvation.

(KELLY *collapses on to* SIOBHAN. *Blackout.*)

ACT TWO

Scene Four

A funeral. One month later.

The same. The sound of a funeral bell tolling. The mannequin stands in a corner, covered by SIOBHAN'S *'Achiever of the Year '94' sash.* SIOBHAN'S *bell sits on a side bench.* CELIA *stands on a side bench looking out.* LUCINDA *sits in her coat, tapping her fingers on the briefcase beside her.*

JEAN *enters. She looks at* LUCINDA, *makes tea drinking and urn switching gesture.* LUCINDA *shakes her head.* JEAN *nods and exits towards the kitchen.*

CLAUDETTE *enters, takes off her coat to reveal her bar manager's uniform. Looks around and exits towards the hall.*

JEAN *re-enters and sits.* CLAUDETTE *re-enters with a chair and decides where to place it.*

CELIA	There's an undertaker over by the gate having a crafty smoke. Wishing that they'd hurry up as his feet are getting cold. Watching the clock. Whistling. Whoever he was, he wasn't short of a few bob. Widow in cashmere. Vicar looking slick. Several Jaeger suits and a top-notch box. Yes. A top-notch box. When I buried my mother we were given three choices. The Balmoral — with brass handles and a name plate — the Windsor — a dark oak stain, and the Buckingham. We plumped for the basic Buckingham. She would have wanted a Buckingham. A no-frills container for a no-frills woman. And on the day the family gathered at those gates and the Vicar greeted us as vicars do but his face fell as the pallbearers set to work. A photographer lurked on the steps. Snaps were being taken for the diocesan magazine. The Vicar peered into the hearse, mumbled something about public

image and market forces — winced at our
chipboard humility — and asked the
photographer to leave. Last time I ever
stepped inside there. The decor cloys
somehow.

(CELIA *steps off the bench and sits.* CLAUDETTE
sits. SIOBHAN *enters from the hall as the bell
stops tolling, grubby and dishevelled with
dirty hair, wearing very tatty clothes. A
silence. All look towards* SIOBHAN.)

SIOBHAN   I'm not late, am I? Four thirty. Your letter —
              it was four thirty, wasn't it? I did what you
              said. I've driven back from the . . . from the
              — I've been to visit — I have been to visit, I
              . . . I'm not late, am I?

              (*A silence.*)

SIOBHAN   Traffic. Terrible. Ice, too. Black ice. Skating
              rink. Anyone else drive? Anyone . . . From
              Siberia this time. Antarctica last time, wasn't
              it? This time it's Siberia. Cold snap. Certainly
              a cold snap. And no grit. No grit on the roads.
              Dangerous. Can't get a grip.

              (*A silence.*)

SIOBHAN   I . . . I'll do anything. Anything you ask me
              to. Anything at all. I'm yours. All yours. You
              just tell me. Tell me what to do. You say
              jump, I'll ask how high. Anything. Anything
              at all.

LUCINDA   Commitment.

              (SIOBHAN *makes her way to a bench.* CLAUDETTE
              *stands and very pointedly pulls out the chair
              for* SIOBHAN. SIOBHAN *sits.*)

SIOBHAN   Oh I see. I see. Hot seat is it? Me in the hot
              seat. Hot seat for . . . not used to it this way
              round, I . . . hot seat. Right. Don't know

where to start. Well. Suppose I do, I . . . not
easy is it? Feel a bit . . . Alright. Alright I'll
. . . I . . . I saw it coming. Simon. Did see it
coming. Simon . . . leaving. Leaving . . . me.
Played on my mind for a while — not that it's
an excuse and I don't want to look back but —
Please try to understand — not an excuse but
. . . I'd loved him for years. Cried for him.
Ached for him before he even noticed me. I
used to eat in his restaurant. I used to eat
everywhere but particularly in his restaurant.
Alone of course. Always I . . . I'd sit in a
corner. Saved my money all week so that come
Saturday night I could afford four courses and
two hours to catch glimpses of him through
the serving hatch. Every week. Regular as
clockwork. I got to know the staff. Head
waiter would open the door for me and say
'Table for Mrs Elvis'. They called me Mrs
Elvis. Mainly because I could eat four courses
and still find room for cheese but also because
of my shoes. My blue suede trainers. Lived in
them. I'd cut a 'V' in the back of each one.
Because of my ankles. My ankles were so huge
that they were all that would fit me. So Mrs
Elvis it was. And I lived for that hole in the
wall. Those little visions of his arms over his
pots and pans. I'd make the meal last as long
as possible then go home feeling like a
beached whale and sob into one of his
napkins. Imagining that he'd touched it.
Trying to smell him. Then it hit me.
Mohammed wasn't going to come to this
mountain. I was going to have to blow the
mountain up. So I bought the books and the
videos and the wall charts and the exercise
machines and I sweated and I went hungry and
I did all the wrong things but the weight fell
away and when I went to the restaurant I ate
less and less until eventually it was just a
starter and a mineral water and one night it
happened. He looked through the serving
hatch and for a moment his eyes stopped on
me. He'd seen me at last. Really seen me. And

I kept going and I got slimmer and slimmer
and his glances got longer and longer until
one night, and I knew it was going to happen,
he came out and asked my opinion on the
menu. And I complimented him and I flirted
with him and then he said, 'Where's Mrs
Elvis? You're sitting in her chair'. And I
reached down to my bag and handed him the
shoes and told him she was gone — gone for
good and he took me by the hand into the
kitchen and he threw the shoes out onto the
fire escape and he kissed me . . . I'd waited
five years for that kiss . . . and I was happy.
We were happy. We were . . . married. Yes.
Married. So I set to work. I was ambitious for
that restaurant. Ambitious for him. Did all his
books. Drummed up business. Streamlined.
Honed. Organised. I like to be organised —
it's good to be organised. I left nothing to
chance. Planning. If you know what's
happening five years down the line, tomorrow
will take care of itself. Yes? I . . . took him in
hand, too. Made sure he was well turned out.
Efficient. But he began to cross me. I'd make
appointments for him and he'd turn up late.
Lay out his blue suit and he'd wear his brown.
Go overdrawn without my . . . terrible row.
Last October. Terrible. Was all set to come
here when I looked through his trouser
pockets and I found a betting slip. Just the
one. He swore it was just a one-off but I was
furious. He hadn't cleared it with me. I do the
books, I — told him, I said 'You develop a
taste for the horses and the business could
sink.' 'Live and let live', he said. Live and let
live. I said what sort of thinking is that — I
said nothing just lives, it has to pay tax and
VAT. 'Where's your sense of humour', he
goes. I said 'I don't find failure very funny,
Simon'. He laughed in my face. Laughed in
my face, turned on his heels and slammed the
door. He spent more and more time at the
restaurant and I spent more time . . . This is
very . . . this was very important to . . . He

couldn't see that it was all for his own good.
His own good. Eventually I thought I'd let him
destroy himself and concentrate on doing what
I do best. Did best — well . . . We hardly saw
each other. And I was happy with that, yes —
I was fine with that — fine — he was driving
me to distraction. He left just before the
Christmas meeting. No big scenes. No dramas.
Just a note. Well I say a note. He wrote 'Good
riddance' in low fat spread on the top of the
freezer. I think he was trying to tell me
something. It worked. I think. I have been
trying. Trying ever since to . . .

LUCINDA   Discipline.

(*A silence.*)

SIOBHAN   All I ever did was try to give you all what you
               wanted.

(CLAUDETTE *turns her back on* SIOBHAN.)

SIOBHAN   Here. I have the money. All of it. The sponsor
               money. And Jean, your fifty . . . I mean I
               didn't have it. But . . . I sold my ring. I had to
               sell my ring.

(SIOBHAN *puts an envelope on the bench.*)

SIOBHAN   The house'll be gone soon. Can't afford the
               payments. Slim for Life have turned their
               backs on me. No job. No home. No husband. I
               hope that gives you some satisfaction.

LUCINDA   Sacrifice.

(*A silence.*)

SIOBHAN   Talk to me. Please. Somebody say something
               please. Why are you all blaming me? Why?

CLAUDETTE   If we hadn't told you to, you wouldn't even
               have visited Kelly would you? Would you?

SIOBHAN   Not terrific with hospitals.

CLAUDETTE   Not terrific with much at all apart from looking after number one.

SIOBHAN   Not made a very good job of that, have I?

CLAUDETTE   And that really cuts to the quick, doesn't it? I knew something was wrong with the girl months ago. You should have known.

SIOBHAN   Maybe if I had she wouldn't be lying on a hospital bed.

CLAUDETTE   Don't throw it on to me, you . . .

JEAN   No. Claudette.

CLAUDETTE   If you set yourself up as some sort of a guru you have to take the responsibility.

SIOBHAN   But what do you expect me to do? What can I do? What more can I do? Tell me.

CELIA   You could start by saying you're sorry, dear. For our sakes.

SIOBHAN   Sorry? Say sorry?

               (*A silence.*)

SIOBHAN   I expected a slap. For her to walk away. Shout at me. But she turned around all pale and she said how will I know when I reach my goal? How will I know when I've achieved? Will I be happy then? And I wanted to take her and shake her and say you stupid, stupid . . . and I thought, what have I done? And it was staring me in the face. And it was me. It was all me. I'm sorry.

               (SIOBHAN *bursts into tears.* LUCINDA *picks up the bell and rings it once.*)

LUCINDA   Realisation. Target. Welcome to the human
                 race.

CLAUDETTE   You've hurt Kelly and you've hurt us. Hurt us
                 all. Very badly.

SIOBHAN   I know. I know. I do know that.

CLAUDETTE   One of us in particular.

SIOBHAN   Rosie. Rosie. Where is Rosie?

CLAUDETTE   Tea break, ladies.

JEAN   Good idea.
CELIA   Yes indeed.
LUCINDA   Absolutely.
SIOBHAN   Oh, oh right. I'll sort the . . .

CLAUDETTE   Where are you going?

SIOBHAN   I thought I'd . . . The urn can be tricky. I've
                 got the knack, I . . .

CLAUDETTE   You sit tight Siobhan. All under control. You
                 just sit tight, sweetheart. OK?

CELIA   I'll give you a hand.

                 (CELIA *and* CLAUDETTE *exit towards the
                 kitchen.* LUCINDA *opens her briefcase and
                 takes out a box of chocolates and puts them
                 on the bench in front of* SIOBHAN.)

LUCINDA   One box of Belgian chocolates.

JEAN   Delicious.

LUCINDA   Truffles. Pralines. All made with fresh cream.
                 Pure luxury. Why don't you open them up
                 Siobhan?

SIOBHAN   Me. You want me to . . .

LUCINDA   Is there a problem?

SIOBHAN   No. No. Anything you say. Anything at all.
                 Really.

                 (SIOBHAN *opens the box slowly.*)

LUCINDA   Amazing the lengths some people will go to to
                 secure a contract. My office is packed with
                 chocolate. Booze. Baskets of fruit. They must
                 think the way to an executive's order book is
                 through her stomach.

JEAN   The job you — Oh well done, Lucinda! That is
                 good news.

SIOBHAN   Congratulations. You . . . you passed that inch
                 test. Achieved that goal.

LUCINDA   I got the job I wanted. That's all.

                 (CLAUDETTE *and* CELIA *enter with tray of tea
                 cups.* CLAUDETTE *carries an empty black bin
                 liner.*)

CLAUDETTE   Here we are then.
LUCINDA   Great.
JEAN   Ah . . .
CELIA   Lovely.

CLAUDETTE   One cup of tea.

                 (SIOBHAN *returns to her chair as* CLAUDETTE
                 hands her a tea cup.)

SIOBHAN   Thank you. Thank you very much. Thank you
                 . . . Oh. Oh I'm sorry, but I don't think I can —

LUCINDA   Not complaining Siobhan, are we?

JEAN   Wouldn't do that. Really wouldn't do that.

SIOBHAN   No. No. It's just . . . it's just . . .

CLAUDETTE   It's just the Co-Op's finest. Silver top milk
                 and two spoonfuls of sugar for good measure.
                 Cheers.

ALL   Cheers.

                    (SIOBHAN *drinks tea and cringes.* LUCINDA *takes
                    the box of chocolates from* SIOBHAN *and hands
                    them to* CLAUDETTE.)

CLAUDETTE   What a fantastic idea.

LUCINDA   I thought so.

CLAUDETTE   Thank you. Hazelnut praline for me.

                    (LUCINDA *takes the box to* JEAN.)

JEAN   Vanilla truffle, I think.

                    (LUCINDA *takes the box to* CELIA.)

CELIA   I'll throw caution to the wind and risk a
                    caramel.

LUCINDA   Cointreau truffle for me. And for Siobhan . . .

                    (LUCINDA *presents the box to* SIOBHAN.)

SIOBHAN   There's at least a hundred and fifty calories in
                    one of these. Not to mention the saturated fat
                    and the . . . coconut cream. Thank you. Thank
                    you.

CLAUDETTE   For what we are about to receive . . .

SIOBHAN   Where is Rosie? Please tell me. Where is . . .

ALL   Cheers.

SIOBHAN   Cheers.

                    (*All eat and relish apart from* SIOBHAN.)

SIOBHAN   Oh well. Forty lengths of the pool and a fruit
                    day for me tomorrow.

                    (*All stare at* SIOBHAN.)

SIOBHAN   Can I have another one?

CLAUDETTE   There's a good girl.

JEAN   Getting there. Definitely getting there.

LUCINDA   Of course you can. Here. And then why don't
                     you pass them around.

SIOBHAN   Yes. Yes of course, I'll . . .

                     (SIOBHAN *takes the box and passes it around.*
                     CLAUDETTE *approaches the mannequin.*)

CLAUDETTE   I think it's about time we got to the bottom of
                     the mysterious mannequin, don't you ladies?

JEAN   ⎫   Oh yes.
CELIA   ⎬   Why not.
LUCINDA   ⎭   Absolutely.

CLAUDETTE   I've been aching to know since day one
                     whether we were talking Saint Mary or
                     Michael. Boy or girl.

                     (CLAUDETTE *wheels the mannequin into the
                     centre of the hall.*)

CLAUDETTE   Let's find out, shall we . . .

SIOBHAN   No.

JEAN   What?

SIOBHAN   It took months, it . . .

LUCINDA   It's already been desecrated.

                     (LUCINDA *pulls the 'achiever' sash from the
                     mannequin, screws it up and throws it to*
                     JEAN.)

LUCINDA   Here Jean — make a perfect duster for your
                     happy home.

SIOBHAN   She isn't . . .

JEAN   Oh but I am, Siobhan. I really truly am.

CLAUDETTE   Lucinda — grab the bin bag.

(LUCINDA *takes the bin liner and opens it up*.)

CLAUDETTE   We start the bidding with a packet of sponge fingers. A large bag of bread sticks and a packet of petits fours. Any takers?

CELIA   Petits fours. Row with Ted. November.

(CLAUDETTE *passes the wrappers to* LUCINDA *who puts them in the bag*.)

LUCINDA   Cherry muffins?

JEAN   October. Justin's tooth extraction.

CLAUDETTE   Bag of lemon bon-bons.

JEAN   Me. Driving test.

CLAUDETTE   Bag of strawberry bon-bons.

JEAN   Me. I failed.

CLAUDETTE   Jaffa Cakes. My Katy's birthday.

LUCINDA   Shortbread fingers. Yearly appraisal.

CLAUDETTE   Orange Matchmakers. Orange Matchmakers. Going . . . going . . .

(SIOBHAN *raises her hand*.)

ALL   Siobhan.

SIOBHAN   December. I'd used the sponsor money to pay off my credit card. Pulled into a service station. Sat in the car park and . . .

CLAUDETTE   One packet of digestive biscuits.

CELIA   Ah — that was me. Rewriting the wills.

LUCINDA   Five kilogram bag of potatoes.

JEAN	Me. Tax return. I had a thing about mash.
CLAUDETTE	One full-fat chocolate-flavoured drink?
SIOBHAN	Came free with a packet of biros. The letters. Chocolate, I . . . Where is Rosie?
CLAUDETTE	Not one. Not two. But three special offer banoffi pies.
CLAUDETTE } LUCINDA	That was me . . . Time of the month. That was me . . . Time of the month.
LUCINDA	Large block of cornish vanilla?
JEAN	Menopause.
CLAUDETTE	Crumpets?
CELIA	Old age.
CLAUDETTE	Packet of custard. Deep dish lasagne.
CLAUDETTE	Cocktail sausages. Mini swiss rolls.
SIOBHAN	Me. Me. Me. I don't know when I . . .
LUCINDA	Let's get the lot off, for God's sake.
LUCINDA } CLAUDETTE	Just pull the . . . Nearly there . . .
	(CLAUDETTE *and* LUCINDA *pull the remaining wrappers from the mannequin until it is bare.*)
SIOBHAN	It's a girl.
CLAUDETTE	No. No it's not . . .
	(CLAUDETTE *extends the vice on the back of the mannequin.*)
CLAUDETTE	Now it's a girl.
	(*A silence.*)
CLAUDETTE	This little lot goes out with the rubbish. Agreed?

           (CLAUDETTE *and* LUCINDA *gather up the*
           wrappers and tie up the bag.)

LUCINDA	Agreed.
CELIA	Only place for it.
JEAN	I think so.

CLAUDETTE   Siobhan. Know where the bins are, don't you?

SIOBHAN   Yes.

CLAUDETTE   Make sure you push it right down to the
                           bottom and screw the lid on tight — OK?

SIOBHAN   OK.

CLAUDETTE   Now there's a good girl.

           (CLAUDETTE *hands the bin bag to* SIOBHAN *and
           she exits towards the hall.*)

LUCINDA   Well.

CELIA   Yes.

LUCINDA   That's the end of that.

CLAUDETTE   Certainly is.

JEAN   Yes.

LUCINDA   Right.

           (*All put their coats on slowly.*)

CLAUDETTE	Funny I . . .
LUCINDA	I suppose we . . .
CELIA	It feels a bit . . .
JEAN	It's been a long . . .

LUCINDA	Sorry I . . .
JEAN	What . . .
CELIA	Oh.
CLAUDETTE	Ha.

(*A silence.*)

CELIA   Well. Back to a lonely hearth for me.

CLAUDETTE   ⎫   Likewise.
LUCINDA   ⎬   Me too.
JEAN   ⎭   Likewise.

LUCINDA   No Ted?

CELIA   No. No. They've gone. To the Pyrenees.
                 George and Ted. Probably scaling the peaks as
                 we speak.

CLAUDETTE   But I thought you . . .

CELIA   I realised I was never going to catch up. Best
                 that — well — they do their thing. I do mine.

JEAN   Gregory's out tutoring. Doing a lot of that
                 right now bless him. Kids are away. Oh well.
                 Long road home.

CLAUDETTE   ⎫   Right.
CELIA   ⎬   I suppose . . .
JEAN   ⎭   Time for the . . .

LUCINDA   Oh for God's sake, lets go round to my flat
                 and open a bottle of wine.

ALL   Yes. Good idea.

LUCINDA   I've given up drinking on my own. Need the
                 company. I'll rustle up some food.

CELIA   ⎫   Sounds enticing.
CLAUDETTE   ⎬   Can chat about Kelly. Visiting and that. Work
                 out a rota or something. She's going to need
                 some help when she leaves hospital, we
                 could . . .

JEAN   We need to discuss this as well . . .

                 (JEAN *picks up the envelope from the bench.*
                 SIOBHAN *enters from the hall.*)

SIOBHAN   What's next?

LUCINDA   (*to* CELIA, JEAN *and* CLAUDETTE) The Vicar's
            been paid, let's go. Time for some fun.

SIOBHAN   Oh lovely. Lovely. Where are we off to? Hang
            on a sec, I'll just get my . . .

            (SIOBHAN *picks up her bag and coat.*)

SIOBHAN   Plenty of room in the car if anyone wants a
            lift. Might as well make the most of it. It goes
            back next week. What? What's the matter?

            (*A silence.*)

SIOBHAN   Oh. I see. That's it, is it?

CLAUDETTE   It was Rosie's choice.

SIOBHAN   Rosie. Where is Rosie? I need to . . .

CLAUDETTE   I'll catch you up.

            (CELIA, LUCINDA *and* JEAN *exit.*)

SIOBHAN   Claudette. Please. I'm begging you. Please.
            Where is she? Where is she? I paid the money
            back. I visited Kelly. Rosie's a good person.
            I'm a bad one and we were friends. We were
            . . . I need her — I need her to forgive me.

CLAUDETTE   She knows that.

SIOBHAN   Oh thank good . . .

CLAUDETTE   But she can't.

SIOBHAN   What? But she's a . . . it's her whole . . .

CLAUDETTE   Faith, yes. It was. But because she can't
            forgive you you've even stolen that from her.

            (CLAUDETTE *exits.*)

SIOBHAN   No. No, I need . . . I NEED HER . . . .

(CELIA *enters, crosses to her scarf on the bench and picks it up.*)

CELIA   Ah — there it is.

(CELIA *steps on to the bench and looks out.*)

CELIA   All done. My undertaker's getting into the hearse. Wiping his nose. Loosening his tie and dreaming of his sausage and chips. Just as it should be. All done now. All . . .

(CELIA *walks past* SIOBHAN *and heads towards the hall exit.*)

SIOBHAN   Not for me. Celia, don't turn your back on me. Please.

CELIA   Oh Siobhan.

SIOBHAN   What about my salvation? Where's my salvation — I want my salvation, too.

(*Blackout.*)

Scene Five

Easter. Two months later.

The sound of bells peeling and 'Jesus Christ Is Risen Today' being played on the organ in the adjacent church. The sound of heavy rain and distant thunder. The room is messy and the mannequin stands covered in a surplice.

CELIA, JEAN *and* CLAUDETTE *stand around the centre bench on which sit plates, cups and a knife. All wear wet weather clothes.* CELIA'S *boots sit next to the centre bench.*

CLAUDETTE *holds a bottle of champagne and* JEAN *holds out tea cups to be filled.*

CLAUDETTE   (*shouting towards the lavatories*) Celia — CELIA — WHAT ON EARTH ARE YOU DOING IN THERE?

(LUCINDA *enters from the kitchen carrying a large cake.*)

LUCINDA   Three thousand calories guaranteed in every mouthful.

JEan   Here. We made a space.
CLAUDETTE }   Well done . . . there you go. The real thing . . .

(CLAUDETTE *opens the champagne.*)

CLAUDETTE   CELIA — COME ON OUT . . . Give me a tea cup — FOUND THE MEANING OF LIFE OR SOMETHING . . .

(CELIA *enters from the direction of the lavatories.* CLAUDETTE *pours champagne.*)

CELIA   Unfortunately not . . . Sorry, I . . .

CLAUDETTE   Happy Easter.

ALL   Happy Easter.

LUCINDA   Shouldn't we have waited?

CLAUDETTE   There's another bottle.

CELIA   What's the time? Does anybody . . .

JEAN   Yes — when is Kelly due here, Claudette?

CLAUDETTE   Any minute now. Had to sort something out with her dad and then she was going to jump into a taxi, so . . .

LUCINDA   You do think this is a good idea? I mean, her coming back here. Bit spooky, isn't it?

CLAUDETTE   It's what she wanted. She's laying her own ghost to rest.

CELIA   We all need the opportunity to do that.

(CELIA *looks out towards the hall.*)

JEAN   She will be . . . I mean . . . She will be — I
            mean . . . She will . . .

CLAUDETTE   She'll be fine. She's a lot stronger. Celia,
            what are you doing?

CELIA   Me? Oh. Nothing. Nothing . . . I was just —
            Ha — nothing. Six months since we first came
            here. Seems like an age ago.

LUCINDA   Same old place. Same dusty old benches. Same
            old feeling.

CELIA   Everything changes but God changes not.

CLAUDETTE   That's not true. There's a new Vicar and
            they've started playing rock music at the
            Sunday service. Was in the paper.

CELIA   God, Claudette. Not the Church of England.
            Two different things entirely.

CLAUDETTE   I've lost weight. This year. Without really
            trying.

LUCINDA   Told you you'd enjoy swimming.

CLAUDETTE   No. It's not that. Just stopped thinking about
            food all the time.

CELIA   That's the trouble with diets. They make you
            fat.

JEAN   Well we're free of all that now.

ALL   Cheers!

            (CLAUDETTE *refills glasses.*)

LUCINDA   One hundred and fifty calories per glass. I can
            still remember the calorie content of
            everything from a pickled walnut to a spoonful
            of caviar. Siobhan's legacy.

CLAUDETTE   Did you call Rosie, Celia?

CELIA   Rosie — what?

CLAUDETTE   You said you'd phone Rosie and . . .

CELIA   Ah — yes. Yes. And I told her we'd all be
               here.

JEAN   I do hope she comes.

LUCINDA   How is she?

CELIA   Needy. Very needy. That's Siobhan's legacy,
               Lucinda. Lovely champagne.

JEAN   Siobhan's house. It's all boarded up you know.

CLAUDETTE   She's probably set herself up with a new
               bunch of disciples somewhere.

CELIA   Oh I don't think so. I don't think so at . . .

               (CELIA *steps on to the bench and looks out.*)

CLAUDETTE   People like her bounce back.

LUCINDA   Celia, I'm sure we'll hear the taxi when it
               arrives.

CELIA   Yes.

LUCINDA   There's no need to keep a lookout.

CELIA   Yes.

LUCINDA   Celia?

CELIA   There's a monster storm brewing. Can see it
               in the distance . . . still raining, too. The new
               Vicar's leading the children in an Easter egg
               roll. Whoops — he's come a cropper. Those
               grass stains'll be a challenge. Funny. That's
               the only thing I'll miss. Taking care of
               someone.

LUCINDA   Celia?

CELIA	The only thing. Isn't that ridiculous?
CLAUDETTE	Is everything alright? With Ted?
CELIA	Everything's fine with Ted. He's a new man. A new man. Huge relief for him. A weight has lifted. He got it all off his chest.
CLAUDETTE	Indigestion?
CELIA	Homosexuality. Ted has discovered he's gay.
CLAUDETTE	Celia!
JEAN	Goodness!
LUCINDA	Must have been a shock.
CELIA	Not really. Knew it was more than a shared interest in plate tectonics that made George and Ted smile. Earth was moving for them alright.
CLAUDETTE	I don't mean to be . . . but he's sixty seven, for God's sake.
CELIA	He's always been a bit backwards in coming forwards. Shame it took him forty years of marriage to work it out. But he got there in the end.
CLAUDETTE	Have you kicked him out?
CELIA	Heavens no. Far too fond of him for that. George is moving in.
LUCINDA	You're very accepting Celia.
JEAN	So all three of you will . . .
CELIA	I may be accepting but I'm not daft. I can live without two blazers to press. No. I am going to spend the nest egg. Live for today. I wanted to travel and I jolly well will travel. So there.

LUCINDA   Room for a small one in your suitcase?

CLAUDETTE   No time for a holiday. You've got your seat on
                the board and your executive chair.

LUCINDA   Not for much longer. I'm chucking it in.

JEAN   You're doing what?

CLAUDETTE   You went through rice cake hell to get that
                job.

LUCINDA   And it wasn't worth it. Why do something I
                hate for the sake of a bigger car? I've spent
                my whole life trying to fit in. It can fit in with
                me now. I'm going to slow down a bit. Take
                some time off. Then maybe college again. I
                took business studies for my parents' sake. It's
                time for me to take whatever I feel like. For
                mine.

CELIA   There's a taxi outside.

CLAUDETTE   The other bottle, I'll — Jean, go and bring her
                in.

CELIA   She looks very well . . .

LUCINDA   Where's my . . .

CLAUDETTE   Celia — get down from up there.

                (JEAN *exits.* CLAUDETTE *finds another bottle of
                champagne.* LUCINDA *finds her camera and
                looks out towards the hall.*)

LUCINDA   She's coming.

                (JEAN *enters with* KELLY, *carrying a large bag.*)

CLAUDETTE   Celia. Come on. She's here.

CELIA   No. No, she isn't.

                (CELIA *steps down from the bench.*)

JEAN	Here we all are . . .

LUCINDA	Hello Kelly.
CELIA	Lovely to see you.
CLAUDETTE	Kelly.

(CLAUDETTE *opens champagne and pours it.*)

CLAUDETTE	Thought we'd have some fizzy wine and cake. No point in being miserable. A sort of . . . a sort of . . .
JEAN	Welcome back party.
CELIA	Welcome forward.
CLAUDETTE	Yes. Welcome forward.
KELLY	Oh my . . .
CELIA	We all wish you well.
LUCINDA	And you look well. You look fantastic.
CLAUDETTE	Everyone got a glass? Good. To Kelly.
ALL	To Kelly.
KELLY	Thanks. Where's Rosie?
CELIA	With us in spirit, dear. Very much with us in spirit.

(KELLY *looks around the hall and spots the mannequin.*)

KELLY	Where's all the . . .
CLAUDETTE	Gone. All happily gone. Dead, buried and forgotten.
KELLY	Good. Good. Well . . .

(*A silence.*)

CLAUDETTE	Cake. Time for the cake.

LUCINDA	Oh yes. Over here Kelly.
CELIA	There's a knife here somewhere.
JEAN	Ah — yes — Claudette — plates . . .

(All gather around the bench. LUCINDA *picks up her camera.)*

LUCINDA   Ladies. This looks like a photo opportunity to me.

(All pose.)

LUCINDA   Say cheese.

CELIA   Cottage or curd, dear?

LUCINDA   Cheddar I think.

ALL   Full-fat cheese!

*(*LUCINDA *takes flash photograph.)*

JEAN   Here. I'll do that.

*(*JEAN *cuts cake into portions.)*

KELLY   Thanks. It meant a lot. Everyone visiting. And . . . just . . . thanks. Sorry — I can't make a speech.

CLAUDETTE   Not required — brought your bag?

KELLY   Yes.

CLAUDETTE   Kelly's moving in with me. Having Katy's room, aren't you sweetheart. If Miss University Challenge deigns to call she can take the couch.

KELLY   Just temporary. 'Til I sort myself out.

CLAUDETTE   You stay as long as you want.

(The bells begin to peel noon.)

CELIA   Oh Lord. Good Lord.

JEAN	Kelly — you're shivering, are you . . .
	(CELIA *steps on to the bench and looks out. The sound of a clap of thunder.*)
LUCINDA	Celia what are you . . .
CELIA	Heavens!
KELLY	It's cold in here. Very cold.
CELIA	Yes it is, Kelly. It's cold, damp and downright horrible so I suggest we all adjourn to the pub. Post haste. Roaring fire and they do a smashing Sunday roast . . .

JEAN   }   Wonderful idea.
LUCINDA   }   Oh yes.
CLAUDETTE }   Why not?

CELIA	You go ahead. Go on. Go — I'll deal with this.
	(*All gather their belongings together.*)
KELLY	I'll take these out.
	(KELLY *picks up tea cups and exits towards kitchen.* CELIA *tidies.*)
CELIA	Off you go.
LUCINDA	I am never coming back in here again.
JEAN	Me neither. Though I may be popping next door some day soon. Gregory and I are doing it at last. We're renewing our vows.

LUCINDA   }   Great.
CLAUDETTE }   See you in a bit, Celia.

JEAN	Yes it is — I think. I hope. I'm not sure. What do you . . .
LUCINDA	Don't ask me, Jean.
JEAN	No. No, I . . .

(LUCINDA, CLAUDETTE *and* JEAN *exit*.)

CELIA   G and T for me, please. Large.

             (KELLY *enters from the kitchen and picks up
             her bag*.)

KELLY   Right.

CELIA   Kelly. I'm delighted you're better. Delighted.
             But don't ever think you'll find everything
             you're looking for in another person. Because
             you won't.

             (CELIA *hands cake box to* KELLY. KELLY *exits*.
             CELIA *steps on to the bench and looks out*.)

CELIA   Good Lord!

             (CELIA *steps off the bench and returns to the
             entrance to the lavatories*.)

CELIA   (*shouting off*) Never send to know for whom
             the bell tolls . . .

             (ROSIE *enters*.)

CELIA   Honestly, Rosie. Subterfuge is exhausting. I
             remember now why I left the WI . . . she's
             coming up the back path with the storm
             behind her. Looking like Lazarus. A vision.

             (CELIA *gathers her belongings together and
             puts on her boots and waterproof clothing*.)

CELIA   You're not unique, you know. Nobody knows
             where they are any more. Nobody. Everything
             used to be so cut and dried. Man was a man,
             woman was a wife — or unfortunate. School.
             Marriage. Children — well, dogs in our case.
             Church. Duty. Now there's nothing. Or
             everything but upside down and utterly corrupt
             and damn confusing. Even Ted. Old stick in
             the mud Ted has been caught up in this 'Who
             the hell am I?' tornado. He's just not sure any

more. Nobody is, Rosie. Nobody is. We all
need some shape. Some consistency. Some
code. We've torn down the pyramid but we
haven't found the circle. And it needs to be
there. It's the edge that holds us together. All
I know is that for me it isn't in there any
more. (*Indicating church.*) And it may not be
out there. But it certainly isn't in here.

(SIOBHAN *enters, dressed in white, looking
stunningly attractive and carrying a large box
beautifully wrapped in white paper.*)

CELIA   The answer doesn't lie in one person. It lies in
             many. So I think I'll take my chances in the
             crowd.

             (CELIA *exits. The sound of thunder.*)

SIOBHAN   Rosie. Rosie.

ROSIE   Siobhan?

SIOBHAN   I can't tell you how happy I am to see you. I . . .

             (SIOBHAN *approaches* ROSIE *with the box.* ROSIE
             retreats. SIOBHAN *places the box on the centre
             bench.*)

SIOBHAN   Celia. Celia, she told me. Told me about you. I
             asked. I've never stopped asking. I wanted to
             know. Rosie. She told me. Told me you don't
             go out. Don't talk to anyone. Told me that
             you've lost all . . .

ROSIE   I didn't want to — don't want to — didn't
             want to see you.

SIOBHAN   I know. But I wanted to see you.

ROSIE   Why?

SIOBHAN   You don't look well.

ROSIE   Fat you mean.

SIOBHAN   Oh, Rosie. Rosie. I mean you don't look well.
             Shadows under your eyes. Grey in your hair.
             It's been hard, hasn't it? Been very hard.
             Come to me sweetheart. Come to . . .

             (SIOBHAN *opens her arms to* ROSIE *and moves
             towards her.* ROSIE *moves away.*)

ROSIE   No.

             (*A sudden clap of thunder and a pool of light
             bursts through the stained glass illuminating a
             bench.*)

ROSIE   What on . . .

SIOBHAN   I'll sit here then. Sit here in the light. Sit here
             at peace, Rosie. Totally at peace. In the light.

             (SIOBHAN *sits on the bench, staring at* ROSIE.)

SIOBHAN   I wish you could feel what I'm feeling, Rosie.
             What I'm feeling right now. Wish you could
             be sitting underneath my skin. Breathing my
             breath. Sharing my peace. So calm. So calm.
             Why don't you come and sit beside me. It's
             warm here. So warm here. In the light.

             (SIOBHAN *stares at* ROSIE. *A silence.*)

SIOBHAN   There's a knife on the table.

ROSIE   What?

SIOBHAN   A knife. On the table. There.

ROSIE   Knife.

SIOBHAN   Why don't you pick it up . . .

ROSIE   What?

SIOBHAN   Pick it up. Go on. Stab me. Rip my heart out.
             Cut me from ear to ear. And you never did
             like what my hairdresser did to you Rosie, so
             why don't you scalp me too.

ROSIE	What do . . .
SIOBHAN	That's what you want to do, isn't it?
ROSIE	No.
SIOBHAN	Because you're so angry.
ROSIE	I'm not . . .
SIOBHAN	Boiling with rage.
ROSIE	How can . . .
SIOBHAN	Can see it in you.
ROSIE	I . . .
SIOBHAN	Fuming, you are.
ROSIE	I . . . I . . .
SIOBHAN	Yes?
ROSIE	I have — have been angry with you.
SIOBHAN	Then kill me.
ROSIE	What do you . . .
SIOBHAN	Because it doesn't matter. Oh Rosie, it doesn't matter what you do. It makes no difference. Not now. Nothing can touch me. Alive or dead I'll still be sitting here. Smiling. In the light.

(*A silence.*)

SIOBHAN	Come to me.
ROSIE	What are . . .
SIOBHAN	Come into the light. You hate me because I was bad . . .
ROSIE	Evil.
SIOBHAN	Such wickedness, yes.
ROSIE	So cruel and . . .

SIOBHAN   Deceit. Lies. The works. Yes. You hate me
               because I was wrong and . . .

ROSIE   So wrong. Wrong about everything.

SIOBHAN   And wrong about Laurence.

               (*A silence*.)

SIOBHAN   Rosie. You hate me because I was wrong about
               Laurence.

ROSIE   No.

SIOBHAN   No?

ROSIE   I hate you because you were right about
               Laurence.

SIOBHAN   I was . . .

ROSIE   Yes.

SIOBHAN   I was . . .

ROSIE   Yes.

SIOBHAN   I was right . . .

ROSIE   Yes. Yes. Yes.

SIOBHAN   Of course I was right.

ROSIE   And he swore.

SIOBHAN   Swore.

ROSIE   On the Bible. I made him — I wanted him to
               tell me the truth. And as soon as his hand
               touched the cover I . . . it slipped away. All
               fell away. Gone. Nothing. I don't believe in
               anyone or any God any more. And I'm lost.
               I'm so lost.

SIOBHAN   Then come into the light. With me.

ROSIE   NO.

(*A loud clap of thunder.* SIOBHAN *stands.*)

SIOBHAN	Oh Rosie. Rosie, I know what you're feeling.
ROSIE	No you can't.
SIOBHAN	I can I can and I do. I've been there too, Rosie. I've been in the pit. I've been in the pit with you.
ROSIE	No.
SIOBHAN	Yes. Oh yes. I've grabbed for walls that aren't there. I've felt myself falling . . .
ROSIE	No. NO.
SIOBHAN	I've thrashed about in the dark . . . .
ROSIE	Don't do this to . . .
SIOBHAN	Me too Rosie. Me too. I've looked into my soul and wished I was blind . . .
ROSIE	Stop . . .
SIOBHAN	And I've seen my own reflection waving at me through a mist. Yes? Yes? Is that how it feels, Rosie? Tell me. Is that how it feels?
ROSIE	I don't know. I don't know anything.
SIOBHAN	Neither did I. Neither did I . . . My sky was black with question marks . . . but in the end the sky cleared and . . . I found the answer. Rosie . . . Rosie I have found the answer. There is an answer.
ROSIE	What. What?
SIOBHAN	Come here. Come closer. I'm holding out my hands to you. Come into the light.
ROSIE	No. No, not this time, not again. I . . .
SIOBHAN	Hope. I'm giving you hope.
ROSIE	No. You're . . .

SIOBHAN   Look at me Rosie. Look at me shining.

ROSIE   Please. Please don't . . .

SIOBHAN   Come into the light.

ROSIE   No.

SIOBHAN   It's here, Rosie. Here. Nectar. The sweetest
                 ether. Heaven itself. It's here for you . . . I
                 know now. I've seen the secret. Share it with
                 me. Please share it with me . . .

                 (SIOBHAN *picks up the box, returns to the light
                 and holds it out towards* ROSIE. ROSIE
                 *approaches slowly and sits at the opposite end
                 of the bench to* SIOBHAN. SIOBHAN *slowly opens
                 the box.*)

SIOBHAN   I've thrown it all away. Cleansed myself.
                 Forgiven myself. The mistakes are gone. The
                 past is gone. I enjoy each moment because I
                 don't think about the last — or the next. It's
                 in the tiny things, Rosie. Hope lives in the
                 tiny things. First find beauty in a grain of
                 sand — don't look at the beach. Touch a
                 single leaf not the whole tree. And eventually
                 Rosie — eventually, when you've loved a
                 single star to perfection you'll see the
                 universe. That star is here. For you — Rosie.
                 Look . . .

                 (SIOBHAN *lifts a large chocolate Easter egg
                 from the box and holds it out towards* ROSIE.)

SIOBHAN   Perfect peace. Perfect joy and perfect . . .

ROSIE   Chocolate.

SIOBHAN   Happiness.

ROSIE   Sin.

SIOBHAN   Happiness. Happiness. Share it with me Rosie.
                 Share it. It's love . . . Love . . . LOVE.

(*A deafening clap of thunder and a flash of
lightning.* SIOBHAN *breaks the egg in half and
a bird on a spring with beak open, eyes ablaze
and wings spread wide leaps urgently skyward
from its centre, then wobbles as it is arrested
on its journey towards the sun.* SIOBHAN *breaks
off some chocolate for* ROSIE *and for herself
and they both eat.* SIOBHAN *walks into the
light.* ROSIE *walks towards her slowly.*)

SIOBHAN   My sun is burning white for you. The
            mystery's waiting to reach into your heart.
            Time to come to me now. Time to touch that
            light . . . this way. Come to me now. This
            way . . .

ROSIE   Is this salvation? Is this my salvation?

SIOBHAN   (*laughing a tinkly laugh*) Oh Rosie, Rosie . . .
            it was wrong. The lifeplan . . . it was wrong.

ROSIE   Wrong? The five stages? The five . . .

SIOBHAN   Oh so very wrong. Because there aren't five
            stages. There are six. Commitment.
            Discipline. Sacrifice. Realisation and
            salvation are just a taste. After the five comes
            the glorious sixth . . .

ROSIE   The sixth . . .

            (ROSIE *almost touches the light.*)

SIOBHAN   Resurrection. Resurrection, Rosie. I have
            achieved resurrection. Time for you to achieve
            resurrection, too.

            (*Blinding white light. Blackout.*)